# easy to make!
# Cupcakes, Muffins & Brownies

# Good Housekeeping

# easy to make!
# Cupcakes, Muffins & Brownies

COLLINS & BROWN

This edition published in Great Britain in 2011
by Collins & Brown
10 Southcombe Street
London W14 0RA

An imprint of Anova Books Company Ltd

The Good Housekeeping website is
www.allaboutyou.com/goodhousekeeping

10 9 8 7 6 5 4 3 2 1

ISBN 978-1-84340-652-5

A catalogue record for this book is available from the British
Library.

Reproduction by Dot Gradations UK, Ltd
Printed and bound by Times Offset, Malaysia

This book can be ordered direct from the publisher at
www.anovabooks.com

## NOTES

- Both metric and imperial measures are given for the recipes. Follow either set of measures, not a mixture of both, as they are not interchangeable.
- All spoon measures are level.
  1 tsp = 5ml spoon; 1 tbsp = 15ml spoon.
- Ovens and grills must be preheated to the specified temperature.
- Use sea salt and freshly ground black pepper unless otherwise suggested.
- Fresh herbs should be used unless dried herbs are specified in a recipe.
- Medium eggs should be used except where otherwise specified. Free-range eggs are recommended.
- Note that certain recipes contain raw or lightly cooked eggs. The young, elderly, pregnant women and anyone with an immune-deficiency disease should avoid these, because of the slight risk of salmonella.
- Calorie, fat and carbohydrate counts per serving are provided for the recipes.
- If you are following a gluten- or dairy-free diet, check the labels on all pre-packaged food goods.
- Recipe serving suggestions do not take gluten- or dairy-free diets into account.

**Picture Credits**
Photographers: Neil Barclay (page 108); Martin Brigdale (pages
89, 120 and 126); Nicki Dowey (pages 32, 33, 36, 37, 38, 40, 56,
80, 81, 82, 84, 85, 86, 88, 92, 93, 96, 98, 100, 101, 103, 104, 105,
106, 107, 109, 110, 111, 112, 114, 115, 117, 121, 122, 123, 124
and 125); Craig Robertson (all Basics photographs); Lucinda
Symons (pages 34, 35, 39, 40, 42, 43, 45, 46, 47, 48, 49, 50, 52,
53, 54, 55, 57, 58, 59, 60, 61, 63, 64, 65, 66, 68, 69, 70, 71, 72,
73, 74, 76, 77, 87, 91, 99 and 116)

Home Economists: Joanna Farrow, Emma Jane Frost, Teresa
Goldfinch, Alice Hart, Lucy McKelvie, Kim Morphew, Bridget
Sargeson and Mari Mererid Williams

Stylists: Wei Tang, Helen Trent and Fanny Ward

# Contents

**0**    **The Basics**    8

**1**    **Cupcakes**    30

**2**    **Muffins and Small Cakes**    78

**3**    **Brownies and Traybakes**    94

**4**    **Biscuits and Cookies**    118

Glossary    127

Index    128

# Foreword

Cooking, for me, is one of life's great pleasures. Not only is it necessary to fuel your body, but it exercises creativity, skill, social bonding and patience. The science behind the cooking also fascinates me, learning to understand how yeast works, or to grasp why certain flavours marry quite so well (in my mind) is to become a good cook.

I've often encountered people who claim not to be able to cook – they're just not interested or say they simply don't have time. My sister won't mind me saying that she was one of those who sat firmly in the camp of disinterested domestic goddess. But things change, she realised that my mother (an excellent cook) can't always be on hand to prepare steaming home-cooked meals and that she actually wanted to become a mother one day who was able to whip up good food for her own family. All it took was some good cook books (naturally, Good Housekeeping was present and accounted for) and some enthusiasm and sure enough she is now a kitchen wizard, creating such confections that even baffle me.

I've been lucky enough to have had a love for all things culinary since as long as I can remember. Baking rock-like chocolate cakes and misshapen biscuits was a rite of passage that I protectively guard. I made my mistakes young, so have lost the fear of cookery mishaps. I think it's these mishaps that scare people, but when you realise that a mistake made once will seldom be repeated, then kitchen domination can start.

This Good Housekeeping Easy to Make! collection is filled with hundreds of tantalising recipes that have been triple tested (at least!) in our dedicated test kitchens. They have been developed to be easily achievable, delicious and guaranteed to work – taking the chance out of cooking.

I hope you enjoy this collection and that it inspires you to get cooking.

*Meike.*

Meike Beck
Cookery Editor
Good Housekeeping

# 0

# The Basics

Getting started

Lining tins

Preparing eggs

Making cakes

Making biscuits and cookies

Using chocolate

Using nuts

Using fruit

Using icing and frosting

Food storage and hygiene

# Getting started

You don't need much specialist equipment for making cakes and cookies; in fact, you probably have many of these items in your kitchen already.

## Weighing and measuring

### Scales

Accurate measurement is essential when baking. The most accurate scale is the electronic type, capable of weighing up to 2kg (4½lb) or 5kg (11lb) in increments of 1–5g. Buy one with a flat platform on which you can put your own bowl or measuring jug, and always remember to set the scale to zero before adding the ingredients.

### Measuring jugs

These can be plastic or glass, and are available in sizes ranging from 500ml (18fl oz) to 2 litres (3½ pints), or even 3 litres (5¼ pints). Have two – a large one and a small one – marked with both metric and imperial measurements.

### Measuring cups

Commonly used in the US, these are used for measuring liquid and dry ingredients. Cups are bought in sets of ¼, ⅓, ½ and 1 cups. A standard 1-cup measure is equivalent to about 250ml (9fl oz).

### Measuring spoons

Useful for the smallest units, accurate spoon measurements go from 1.25ml (¼ tsp) to 15ml (1 tbsp).

# Mixing

## Bowls

For mixing large quantities, such as cake mixtures, you will need at least two large bowls, including one with a diameter of up to 38cm (15in).

- Plastic or glass bowls are best if you need to use them in the microwave.
- Steel bowls with a rubber foot will keep their grip on the worksurface.
- Bowls with gently tapered sides – much wider at the rim than at the base – are useful for mixing dough.

## Spoons

For general mixing, the cheap and sturdy wooden spoon still can't be beaten, but equivalents made from thermoplastic materials are heatproof and may suit you better. A large metal spoon for folding ingredients together is also invaluable when baking.

# Bakeware

As well as being thin enough to conduct heat quickly and efficiently, bakeware should be sturdy enough not to warp when heated. Most bakeware is made from aluminium, and it may have enamel or non-stick coatings.

**Cake tins** Available in many shapes and sizes, tins may be single-piece, loose-based or springform.
**Loaf tins** Available in various sizes, one of the most useful is a 900g (2lb) tin.
**Pie tins and muffin tins** You should have both single-piece tins and loose-based tins for flans and pies.
**Oven-safe silicone** is safe to touch straight from the oven, is inherently non-stick and is also flexible – making it easy to remove muffins and other bakes.

> ### Other useful utensils
> Baking sheets (two)
> Spatulas
> Wire whisks
> Fine sieve
> Microplane grater
> Rolling pin
> Thin skewers
> Cookie cutters

# Electrical equipment

**Food processor** For certain tasks, such as making breadcrumbs or pastry or for chopping large quantities of nuts, food processors are unbeatable. Most come with a number of attachments – dough hooks, graters, slicers – which are worth having, even if only for occasional use.
**Blender** These are less versatile than food processors, but unmatched for certain tasks, such as puréeing fruit. The traditional jug blender is great but some cooks prefer a hand-held stick blender, which can be used directly in a pan, bowl or jug.
**Freestanding mixer** An electric mixer may be a good investment if you do a lot of baking, but decide first whether you have space in your kitchen. They are big and heavy to store.
**Hand-held electric whisk** Useful for creaming together butter and sugar in baking and for making meringues. They don't take up a lot of space and can be packed away easily.

**2**

**5**

# Lining tins

When making cakes, you usually need to grease and/or line the tin with greaseproof paper before filling it with cake mixture. Lightly grease the tin first to help keep the paper in place. You will need to use different techniques according to the shape of the tin.

## Round tin

**1** Put the tin on a sheet of greaseproof paper and draw a circle around its circumference. Cut out the circle just inside the drawn line.

**2** Cut a strip or strips about 2cm (³/₄in) wider than the depth of the tin and fold up one long edge of each strip by 1cm (¹/₂in). Make cuts, about 2.5cm (1in) apart, through the folded edge of the strip(s) up to the fold line.

**3** Lightly grease the tin with butter, making sure it is completely coated.

**4** Press the strip(s) on to the sides of the tin so that the snipped edge sits on the base.

**5** Lay the circle in the bottom of the tin and grease the paper.

## Swiss roll tin

Use this method for Swiss roll or other shallow baking tins.

**1** Lightly grease the tin with butter, making sure it is completely coated.

**2** Cut a piece of baking parchment into a rectangle 7.5cm (3in) wider and longer than the tin. Press it into the tin and cut at the corners, then fold to fit neatly. Grease all over.

**2**

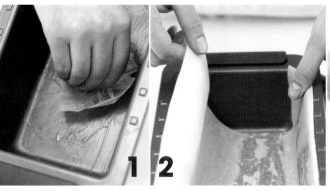

## Loaf tin

**1** Lightly grease the tin with butter, making sure it is completely coated.

**2** Cut out a sheet of greaseproof paper to the same length as the base and wide enough to cover both the base and the long sides. Press it into position, making sure that it sits snugly in the corners.

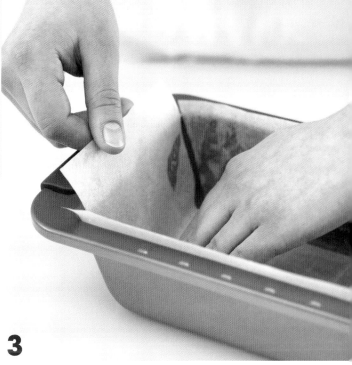

**3** Now cut another sheet to the same width as the base and long enough to cover both the base and the ends of the tin. Press into place. Grease the paper all over.

## Square tin

**1** Cut out a square of greaseproof paper slightly smaller than the base of the tin. Cut four strips about 2cm (³/₄in) wider than the depth of the tin and fold up one of the longest edges of each strip by 1cm (¹/₂in).

**2** Lightly grease the tin with butter, making sure it is coated on all sides and in the corners.

**3** Cut one strip to the length of the side of the tin and press into place in one corner then along the length of the strip with the narrow folded section sitting on the base. Continue, cutting to fit into the corners, to cover all four sides.

**4** Lay the square on the base of the tin, then grease the paper, taking care not to move the side strips.

## Cracking and separating

You'll need to separate eggs for making meringues and some cakes. It's easy, but it requires care. If you're separating more than one egg, break each one into an individual cup. Separating them individually means that if you break one yolk, you won't spoil the whole batch. Keeping the whites yolk-free is particularly important for techniques such as whisking.

**1** Crack the egg more carefully than usual: right in the middle to make a break between the two halves that is just wide enough to get your thumbnail into.

**2** Holding the egg over a bowl with the large end pointing down, carefully lift off the small half. Some of the white will drip and slide into the bowl while the yolk sits in the large end of the shell.

**3** Carefully slide the yolk into the smaller end, then back into the large end to allow the remaining white to drop into the bowl. Take care not to break the yolk; even a speck can stop the whites from whisking up.

# Preparing eggs

Mastering three simple techniques – cracking, separating and whisking – will make every aspect of baking easier.

### How can I tell if my eggs are fresh?

A fresh egg should feel heavy in your hand and will sink to the bottom of the bowl or float on its side when put into water (1). Older eggs, over two weeks old, will float vertically (2).

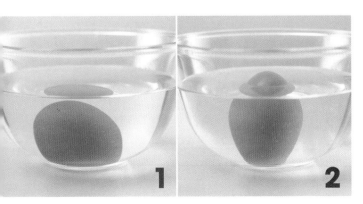

# Whisking

**1** Use a hand-held electric whisk or a wire whisk. Make sure that there is no trace of yolk in the whites and that the whisk and bowl are clean and dry. At a low speed, use the whisk in a small area of the whites until it starts to become foamy.

**2** Increase the speed and work the whisk through the whites until glossy and soft rounded peaks form. Do not over-whisk as the foam will become dry and grainy.

# Meringues

Baking meringues is best done whenever you know you won't be needing your oven for a good few hours, as they must be left to dry in the turned-off oven for several hours.

**To make 12 meringues, you will need:**
3 medium egg whites, 175g (6oz) caster sugar.

**1** Preheat the oven to 170°C (150°C fan oven) mark 3. Cover a baking sheet with baking parchment. Put the egg whites into a large, clean, grease-free bowl.

**2** Whisk them until soft peaks form. Add a spoonful of sugar and whisk until glossy.

**3** Keep adding the sugar a spoonful at a time, whisking thoroughly after each addition until you have used half the sugar. The mixture should be thick and glossy.

**4** Sprinkle the remaining sugar over the mixture and then gently fold in using a metal spoon.

**5** Hold a dessertspoon in each hand and pick up a spoonful of mixture in one spoon, then scrape the other one against it to lift the mixture off. Repeat the process a few times, to form a rough oval shape. Using the empty spoon, push the oval on to the baking sheet; hold it just over the sheet so that it doesn't drop from a great height. Continue this process with the remaining mixture to make 12 meringues.

**6** Put the meringues in the oven and bake for 15 minutes, then turn the oven off and leave them in the oven to dry out for several hours or overnight.

## Creaming

A classic creamed (Victoria) sponge can be used to make many types of cake, including chocolate or fruit.

**1** Put the butter and sugar in a bowl and beat with a hand-held electric whisk or wooden spoon until pale, soft and creamy.

**2** Beat the eggs in a separate bowl and gradually add to the butter and sugar mixture, beating well until the mixture is thick and of dropping consistency. If you like, add a spoonful of flour while adding the eggs to prevent curdling.

**3** Gently fold in the remaining flour using a large metal spoon or spatula, then spoon the mixture into the prepared tin(s), level the surface and bake.

# Making cakes

Many of the cakes and bakes in this book use one of these basic techniques: creaming, whisking, all-in-one.

## Whisking

**1** Melt the butter in a small pan. Put the eggs and sugar in a large bowl set over a pan of simmering water. Whisk for about 5 minutes with an electric hand mixer until creamy and pale and the mixture leaves a trail when you lift the whisk.

**2** Gently fold half the flour into the mixture. Pour the butter around the edge of the mixture, then fold in the remaining flour and butter. Pour into the prepared tin(s) and bake.

## All-in-one

**1** Put the butter, sugar, eggs, flour and baking powder in a large bowl or mixer.

**2** Using a hand-held electric whisk, mix slowly to start, then increase the speed slightly until well combined. Fold in any remaining ingredients, such as milk or fruit, then spoon into the prepared tin(s) and bake.

### Testing fruit cakes

**1** To test if a fruit cake is cooked, insert a skewer into the centre of the cake, leave for a few moments, then pull it out. If it comes away clean, the cake is ready.

**2** If any mixture sticks to the skewer, the cake is not quite done, so put the cake back in the oven for a few more minutes, then test again with a clean skewer.

### Testing sponges

**1** Gently press the centre of the sponge. It should feel springy. If it's a whisked cake, it should be just shrinking away from the sides of the tin.

**2** If you have to put it back into the oven, close the door gently so that the vibrations don't cause the cake to sink in the centre.

### Troubleshooting: fruit cake
**A dense texture** may be due to too little raising agent, or adding the eggs too quickly.
**A peaked, cracked top** may form if the oven is too hot or the cake is too near the top of the oven; the tin is too small; or too much raising agent was used.

### Cooling cakes
**Sponge cakes** should be taken out of their tins soon after baking. Invert on to a wire rack covered with sugar-dusted baking parchment.
**Leave fruit cakes** to cool in the tin for 15 minutes before turning out.
**Allow rich fruit cakes** to cool completely before turning out; there is a risk of breaking otherwise.

# Making biscuits and cookies

Home-made biscuits are always welcome; the only drawback is they are so moreish – you'll need all your willpower to stay away from the biscuit tin.

## Cookie troubleshooting

Although very simple in their composition, biscuits can be surprisingly prone to baking problems because they cook so quickly. It's as well to be aware of the possible problems and to know what can cause them. Following a few key points should minimise most of the risks and potential pitfalls.

**Use** a shiny-based baking sheet; a darker-coloured sheet will absorb a greater amount of heat and can therefore burn the undersides of the biscuits.

**Don't** overcrowd the biscuits on the baking sheet or in the oven – air needs to circulate all around them. If you are baking more than one sheet, make sure they are on shelves at least 20.5cm (8in) apart.

**Turn** the baking sheet(s) around once or twice during baking. Most ovens get hotter in some places than in others, and this can cause uneven cooking.

**If you** are cooking more than one sheet, be prepared to have them bake at different speeds. Watch them closely for uneven cooking.

**Start** testing biscuits slightly before you expect them to be cooked. And watch them very closely during the final minutes, as they can go from perfect to overcooked in a matter of only a few seconds.

**Like cakes,** biscuits must be transferred to a wire rack while they are still hot. The hot baking sheet will continue to cook them, and steam will build up underneath, which can make the bases soggy. As soon as they are cooked, lift the biscuits from the baking sheet and transfer to a wire rack to cool. Some biscuits, however (particularly those made with syrup), need to be left on the baking sheet to firm up a little before they are transferred to a rack.

**Ideally,** cool the biscuits on a fairly fine-meshed rack.

**If possible,** raise the rack by putting it on supports so that it is at least a few centimetres higher than the worksurface underneath: the more air circulating underneath, the crisper the bases will be.

**If the biscuits** are tough or dry, the dough may have been overworked or too much flour may have been added.

**Biscuits** that spread too much during baking contain too much butter or sugar, or the mixture may have been overbeaten.

**A cake-like** texture indicates that too much flour was used or the biscuits were baked at too high a temperature.

# Rolled Vanilla Biscuits

The easiest way to make biscuits of consistent thickness is by rolling and then cutting using a biscuit cutter. The dough must be firm enough to roll to a thickness of 3mm ($\frac{1}{8}$in).

**To make 48 biscuits, you will need:**
175g (6oz) softened unsalted butter, 200g (7oz) golden caster sugar, 350g (12oz) plain flour, 1 medium egg, 2 tsp vanilla bean paste, 2 tbsp golden icing sugar.

**1** Preheat the oven to 200°C (180°C fan oven) mark 6. Put the butter, caster sugar, flour, egg and vanilla paste into a food processor and whiz to combine. Alternatively, cream the butter and sugar, and then stir in the flour, egg and vanilla.

**2** Put the dough on a large sheet of baking parchment. Press the dough gently but firmly with the palm of your hand to flatten it slightly, then put another sheet of baking parchment on top – this will prevent the dough from sticking.

**3** Use a rolling pin to roll out the dough to 3mm ($\frac{1}{8}$in) thick, and then remove the top sheet of baking parchment.

**4** Using 6.5cm ($2\frac{1}{2}$in) cutters, stamp out biscuits, leaving a 3mm ($\frac{1}{8}$in) gap between each one.

**5** Peel off the trimmings around the shapes, then slide the baking parchment and biscuits on to a flat baking sheet.

**6** Re-roll the trimmings between two new sheets of baking parchment, then stamp out shapes as before and slide on to another baking sheet.

**7** Bake the biscuits for 10–12 minutes until pale golden. Cool for a few minutes, then transfer to a wire rack to cool completely.

**8** Dust the biscuits with sifted icing sugar. Store in an airtight container for up to five days.

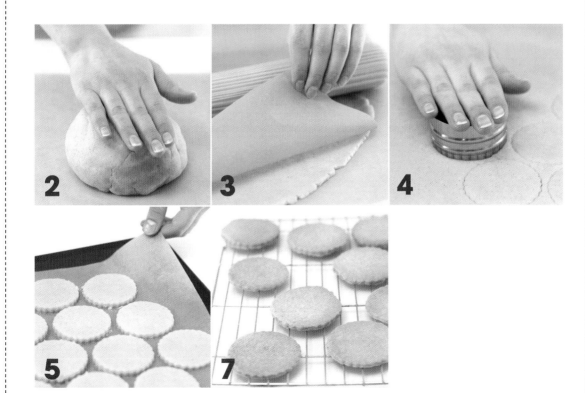

## Shaving

This is the easiest decoration of all because it doesn't call for melting the chocolate.

**1** Hold a chocolate bar upright on the worksurface and shave pieces off the edge with a swivel peeler.

**2** Alternatively, grate the chocolate, against a coarse or medium-coarse grater, to make very fine shavings.

### Cook's Tip

**When melting chocolate,** always use a gentle heat. Make sure the base of the bowl is not touching the water. However tempting, only stir the chocolate once or twice until it has melted: overstirring will make it thicken into a sticky mess.
**Don't** let water or steam touch the chocolate or it will 'seize' – become hard and unworkable. If it has seized, you can try saving it by stirring in a few drops of flavourless vegetable oil.

# Using chocolate

As well as being a delicious ingredient in many cakes and bakes, chocolate can be used to make stunning decorations.

### Which chocolate to choose?
The type of chocolate you choose will have a dramatic effect on the end product. For the best results, buy chocolate that has a high proportion of cocoa solids, preferably at least 70%. Most supermarkets stock a selection. At the top end of the scale, couverture chocolate is preferred by chefs for confectionery work and gives an intense chocolate flavour; it is probably best reserved for special mousses and gâteaux. It is available in milk, plain and white varieties from specialist chocolate shops.

# Melting

For cooking or making decorations, chocolate is usually melted first.

**1** Break the chocolate into pieces and put in a heatproof bowl or in the top of a double boiler. Set over a pan of gently simmering water.

**2** Heat very gently until the chocolate starts to melt, then stir only once or twice until completely melted.

# Chocolate curls

**1** Melt the chocolate, as above, and spread it out in a thin layer on a marble slab or clean worksurface. Leave to firm up.

**2** Use a sharp blade (such as a pastry scraper, a cook's knife or a very stiff spatula) to scrape through the chocolate at a 45-degree angle. The size of the curls will be determined by the width of the blade.

# Chocolate leaves

**1** Wash and dry some rose or bay leaves. Spread slightly cooled melted chocolate in a thin, even layer over the shiny side of the leaf. Spread it right out to the edge using a paintbrush, but wipe off any chocolate that drips over the edge.

**2** Leave to cool completely. Then, working very gently and carefully, peel the leaf off the chocolate.

## Blanching and skinning

After nuts have been shelled, they are still coated with a skin, which, although edible, tastes bitter. This is easier to remove if the nuts are blanched.

**1** Put the shelled nuts in a bowl and cover with boiling water. Leave for 2 minutes, then drain.

**2** Remove the skins by rubbing the nuts in a teatowel or squeezing between your thumb and index finger.

# Using nuts

Nuts are used in many cakes and cookies. Some can be bought ready-prepared, but there are various tips and techniques that may be helpful.

## Toasting

Toasting nuts also makes their skins easier to remove, as well as improving the flavour.

**1** Preheat the oven to 200°C (180°C fan oven) mark 6. Put the shelled nuts on a baking sheet in a single layer, and bake for 8–15 minutes until the skins are lightly coloured.

**2** Remove the skins by rubbing the nuts in a teatowel.

## Chopping

Unless you want very large pieces, the easiest way to chop nuts is in the food processor. Alternatively, place a chopping board on a folded teatowel on the worksurface and use a cook's knife. Only chop about 75g (3oz) of nuts at a time. **Note:** Allow nuts to cool completely after skinning and before chopping.

**1** Put the nuts in a food processor and pulse at 10-second intervals.

**2** Chop to the size of coarse breadcrumbs. Store in an airtight container for up to two weeks.

---

**Storing nuts**

Because of their high fat content, nuts do not keep particularly well and turn rancid if kept for too long. **Always** buy nuts from a shop with a high turnover of stock so you know they're likely to be fresh. **Store** in an airtight container in a cool, dark place, or in the refrigerator, and use well within the 'best before' date on the pack.

---

## Slicing and slivering

Although you can buy sliced and slivered nuts, it's easy enough to make your own.

**1** To slice, put the nuts on a board. Using a cook's knife, carefully slice the nuts as thinly as required.

**2** To make slivers, carefully cut the slices to make narrow matchsticks.

## Decorating with fruit

Fresh seasonal fruit makes an attractive decoration, either singly or arranged with other fruit. In summer, berries such as strawberries, raspberries and blueberries make an excellent choice. Slice or halve strawberries if you like. You can also use chopped mango and whole redcurrants or sliced kiwi fruit and halved seedless grapes or orange segments.

## Zesting

**Most citrus fruit** is sprayed with wax and fungicides or pesticides. Unless you buy unwaxed fruit, wash it with a tiny drop of washing-up liquid and warm water, then rinse with clean water and dry thoroughly on kitchen paper.
**To use a grater,** rub the fruit over the grater, using a medium pressure to remove the zest without removing the white pith.
**To use a zester,** press the blade into the citrus skin and run it along the surface to take off long shreds.

# Using fruit

Citrus fruit is an important flavouring: the grated zest and juice of oranges and lemons are used in many cake mixtures and icings. Other fruit may be used as an ingredient or a colourful, fresh-tasting decoration.

# Slicing apples

Core and peel the apple, then cut in half.
**For flat slices,** hold the apple cut side down and slice
with the knife blade parallel to the hollow left by the core.
**For crescent-shaped slices,** stand the fruit on its end and
cut slices into the hollow as if you were slicing a pie.

# Segmenting citrus fruits

**1** Cut off a slice at both ends of the fruit, then cut off
the peel, just inside the white pith.

**2** Hold the fruit over a bowl to catch the juice and cut
between the segments just inside the membrane to
release the flesh. Continue until all the segments are
removed. Squeeze the juice from the membrane into
the bowl and use as required.

# Hulling strawberries

**1** Wash the strawberries gently and dry on kitchen
paper.

**2** Remove the hull (the centre part that was attached
to the plant) from the strawberry using a strawberry
huller or a small, sharp knife. Put the knife into the
small, hard area beneath the green stalk and gently
rotate to remove a small, cone-shaped piece.

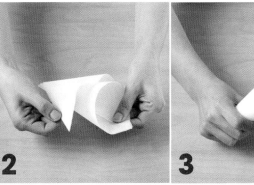

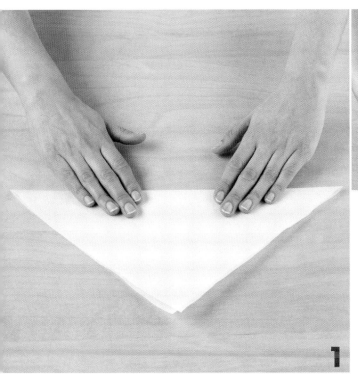

# Using icing and frosting

## Piping bags

Piping bags can be bought from specialist cake decorating shops, or you can make your own from greaseproof paper. A bag with a very small hole will allow you to make delicate patterns or writing; larger holes are more suitable for textured effects on the cake surface.

**1** Cut a piece of greaseproof paper about 20.5cm (8in) square. Fold in half diagonally.

**2** Bring the two corners of the long side of the triangle up to meet the top of the triangle, one in front of it and one behind, to make a cone.

**3** Holding all three corners of the triangle together firmly, make sure the tip of the cone is closed, then fold over the corners and pinch all around the top of the cone to secure. Snip off the tip. Fill with icing and test the thickness of the line on a piece of baking parchment.

# Icings and Frostings

## Glacé Icing

225g (8oz) icing sugar
few drops of vanilla extract (optional)
few drops of food colouring (optional)

**makes** 225g (8oz)
**preparation** 5 minutes

**1** Sift the icing sugar into a bowl. Add a few drops of vanilla extract, if you like.

**2** Using a wooden spoon, gradually stir in 2–3 tbsp hot water until the mixture is the consistency of thick cream. Beat until white and smooth and the icing is thick enough to coat the back of the spoon. Add colouring if you like, and use straightaway.

### Cook's Tip

This quantity is sufficient to cover the top of one large sandwich cake, or about 16 small cakes.

### Try Something Different

**Orange or Lemon Glacé Icing**
Replace the water with strained orange or lemon juice.
**Chocolate Glacé Icing**
Sift 2 tsp cocoa powder with the icing sugar.
**Coffee Glacé Icing**
Flavour the icing with 1 tsp coffee essence or 2 tsp instant coffee granules dissolved in 1 tbsp of hot water.

## Vanilla Frosting

150g (5oz) icing sugar, sifted
5 tsp vegetable oil
1 tbsp milk
a few drops of vanilla extract

**makes** about 175g (6oz)
**preparation** 5 minutes

Put the icing sugar in a bowl and beat in the oil, milk and vanilla extract until smooth.

## Buttercream

75g (3oz) unsalted butter, softened
175g (6oz) icing sugar, sifted
few drops of vanilla extract
1–2 tbsp milk or water

**makes** 250g (9oz)
**preparation** 5 minutes

**1** Put the butter into a bowl and beat with a wooden spoon until it is light and fluffy.

**2** Gradually stir in the icing sugar, vanilla extract and milk. Beat well until light and smooth.

### Cook's Tip

This quantity is sufficient to cover the top of a 20.5cm (8in) cake. To make enough to cover the top and sides, increase the quantities by one-third.

### Try Something Different

**Orange, Lime or Lemon Buttercream**
Replace the vanilla extract with a little finely grated orange, lime or lemon zest. Add 1–2 tbsp juice from the fruit instead of the milk, beating well to avoid curdling the mixture. If the mixture is to be piped, omit the zest.
**Chocolate Buttercream**
Blend 1 tbsp cocoa powder with 2 tbsp boiling water and cool before adding to the mixture.
**Coffee Buttercream**
Replace the vanilla extract with 2 tsp instant coffee granules dissolved in 1 tbsp boiling water; cool before adding to the mixture.

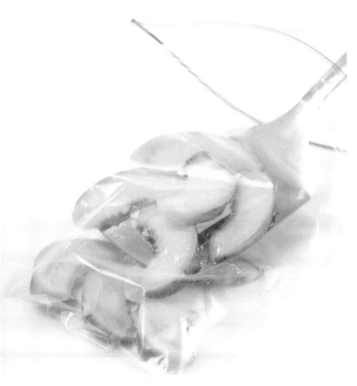

# Food storage and hygiene

Storing food properly and preparing food in a hygienic way is important to ensure that food remains as nutritious and flavourful as possible, and to reduce the risk of food poisoning.

## Hygiene

When you are preparing food, always follow these important guidelines:

**Wash your hands thoroughly** before handling food and again between handling different types of food, such as raw and cooked meat and poultry. If you have any cuts or grazes on your hands, be sure to keep them covered with a waterproof plaster.

**Wash down worksurfaces regularly** with a mild detergent solution or multi-surface cleaner.

**Use a dishwasher if available.** Otherwise, wear rubber gloves for washing-up, so that the water temperature can be hotter than unprotected hands can bear. Change drying-up cloths and cleaning cloths regularly. Note that leaving dishes to drain is more hygienic than drying them with a teatowel.

**Keep pets out of the kitchen** if possible; or make sure they stay away from worksurfaces. Never allow animals on to worksurfaces.

## Shopping

Always choose fresh ingredients in prime condition from stores and markets that have a regular turnover of stock to ensure you buy the freshest produce possible.

**Make sure** items are within their 'best before' or 'use by' date. (Foods with a longer shelf life have a 'best before' date; more perishable items have a 'use by' date.)

**Pack frozen** and chilled items in an insulated cool bag at the check-out and put them into the freezer or refrigerator as soon as you get home.

**During warm weather** in particular, buy perishable foods just before you return home. When packing items at the check-out, sort them according to where you will store them when you get home – the refrigerator, freezer, storecupboard, vegetable rack, fruit bowl, etc. This will make unpacking easier – and quicker.

# The storecupboard

Although storecupboard ingredients will generally last a long time, correct storage is important:

**Always check packaging** for storage advice – even with familiar foods, because storage requirements may change if additives, sugar or salt have been reduced. Check storecupboard foods for their 'best before' or 'use by' date and do not use them if the date has passed.

**Keep all food cupboards scrupulously clean** and make sure food containers and packets are properly sealed.

**Once opened, treat canned foods as though fresh.** Always transfer the contents to a clean container, cover and keep in the refrigerator. Similarly, jars, sauce bottles and cartons should be kept chilled after opening. (Check the label for safe storage times after opening.)

**Transfer dry goods** such as sugar, rice and pasta to moisture-proof containers. When supplies are used up, wash the container well and thoroughly dry before refilling with new supplies.

**Store oils in a dark cupboard** away from any heat source as heat and light can make them turn rancid and affect their colour. For the same reason, buy olive oil in dark green bottles.

**Store vinegars in a cool place;** they can turn bad in a warm environment.

**Store dried herbs, spices and flavourings** in a cool, dark cupboard or in dark jars. Buy in small quantities as their flavour will not last indefinitely.

**Store flours and sugars** in airtight containers.

# Refrigerator storage

Fresh food needs to be kept in the cool temperature of the refrigerator to keep it in good condition and discourage the growth of harmful bacteria. Store day-to-day perishable items, such as opened jams and jellies, mayonnaise and bottled sauces, in the refrigerator along with eggs and dairy products, fruit juices, bacon, fresh and cooked meat (on separate shelves), and salads and vegetables (except potatoes, which don't suit being stored in the cold). A refrigerator should be kept at an operating temperature of 4–5°C.

It is worth investing in a refrigerator thermometer to ensure the correct temperature is maintained. To ensure your refrigerator is functioning effectively for safe food storage, follow these guidelines:

**To avoid bacterial cross-contamination,** store cooked and raw foods on separate shelves, putting cooked foods on the top shelf. Ensure that all items are well wrapped.

**Never put hot food** into the refrigerator, as this will cause the internal temperature of the refrigerator to rise.

**Avoid overfilling** the refrigerator, as this restricts the circulation of air and prevents the appliance from working properly.

**It can take some time** for the refrigerator to return to the correct operating temperature once the door has been opened, so don't leave it open any longer than is necessary.

**Clean the refrigerator regularly,** using a specially formulated germicidal refrigerator cleaner. Alternatively, use a weak solution of bicarbonate of soda: 1 tbsp to 1 litre (1³/₄ pints) water.

**If your refrigerator** doesn't have an automatic defrost facility, defrost regularly.

**For pre-packed foods,** always adhere to the 'use by' date on the packet.

# 1

# Cupcakes

Chocolate Cupcakes

Fairy Cakes

Lavender and Honey Cupcakes

St Clements Cupcakes

Kitten Cupcakes

Sour Cherry Cupcakes

Vanilla and White Chocolate Cupcakes

Orange and Poppy Seed Cupcakes

Cookies and Cream Cupcakes

Dainty Cupcakes

Coconut and Lime Cupcakes

Toast and Marmalade Cupcakes

Pavlova Cupcakes

Cherry Bakewell Cupcakes

Sticky Gingerbread Cupcakes

Apple Crumble Cupcakes

Coffee Walnut Whip Cupcakes

Raspberry Ripple Cupcakes

The Ultimate Carrot Cupcakes

Be Mine Cupcakes

Rocky Road Cupcakes

Peanut Butter Cupcakes

Red Nose Buns

Polka Dot Cupcakes

Mango and Passion Fruit Cupcakes

Gluten-free Pistachio and Polenta Cupcakes

Mallow Madness Cupcakes

Breakfast Cupcakes

Mini Green Tea Cupcakes

Sweet Shop Cupcakes

Easter Cupcakes

Truffle Kisses Cupcakes

Honeycomb Cream Cupcakes

Nutty Cupcakes

Jewelled Cupcakes

Secret Garden Cupcakes

Aniseed Cupcakes

Banoffee Cupcakes

Pretty Pink Cupcakes

Marbled Chocolate Cupcakes

Sea Breeze Cupcakes

## Freezing Tip

**To freeze** Complete the recipe to the end of step 3.
Open-freeze, then wrap and freeze.
**To use** Thaw for about 1 hour, then complete the recipe.

125g (4oz) unsalted butter, softened

125g (4oz) light muscovado sugar

2 medium eggs, beaten

15g (½oz) cocoa powder

100g (3½oz) self-raising flour

100g (3½oz) plain chocolate
(at least 70% cocoa solids), roughly chopped

# Chocolate Cupcakes

### TOPPING

150ml (¼ pint) double cream

100g (3½oz) plain chocolate
(at least 70% cocoa solids), broken up

**1** Preheat the oven to 190°C (170°C fan oven) mark 5. Line a 12-hole and a 6-hole bun tin or muffin tin with paper muffin cases.

**2** Beat the butter and sugar together until light and fluffy. Gradually beat in the eggs. Sift the cocoa powder with the flour and fold into the creamed mixture with the chopped chocolate. Divide the mixture among the paper cases and lightly flatten the surface with the back of a spoon.

**3** Bake for 20 minutes, then transfer to a wire rack and leave to cool completely.

**4** For the topping, put the cream and chocolate into a heavy-based pan over a low heat and heat until melted, then allow to cool and thicken slightly. Spoon on to the cooled cakes, then stand the cakes upright on the wire rack and leave for 30 minutes to set.

| Serves | EASY | | NUTRITIONAL INFORMATION |
|---|---|---|---|
| | **Preparation Time** | **Cooking Time** | **Per Cupcake** |
| **18** | 15 minutes | 25 minutes, plus cooling and setting | 203 calories; 14g fat (of which 8g saturates); 19g carbohydrate; 0.2g salt |

### Freezing Tip

**To freeze** Complete the recipe to the end of step 3. Open-freeze, then wrap and freeze.
**To use** Thaw for about 1 hour, then complete the recipe.

### Try Something Different

**Chocolate Fairy Cakes:** Replace 2 tbsp of the flour with the same amount of cocoa powder. Stir 50g (2oz) chocolate chips, sultanas or chopped dried apricots into the mixture at the end of step 1. Complete the recipe.

# Fairy Cakes

125g (4oz) self-raising flour, sifted
1 tsp baking powder
125g (4oz) caster sugar
125g (4oz) unsalted butter, very soft
2 medium eggs
1 tbsp milk

**ICING AND DECORATION**
225g (8oz) icing sugar, sifted
assorted food colourings (optional)
sweets, sprinkles or coloured sugar

**1** Preheat the oven to 200°C (180°C fan oven) mark 6. Put paper cases into 18 of the holes in 2 bun tins.

**2** Put the flour, baking powder, sugar, butter, eggs and milk into a mixing bowl and beat with a hand-held electric whisk for 2 minutes or until the mixture is pale and very soft. Half-fill each paper case with the mixture.

**3** Bake for 10–15 minutes until golden brown. Transfer to a wire rack and leave to cool completely.

**4** Put the icing sugar into a bowl and gradually blend in 2–3 tbsp warm water until the icing is fairly stiff, but spreadable. Add a couple of drops of food colouring, if you like.

**5** When the cakes are cold, spread the tops with the icing and decorate.

| EASY | | NUTRITIONAL INFORMATION | Serves |
|---|---|---|---|
| **Preparation Time** 20 minutes | **Cooking Time** 10–15 minutes, plus cooling and setting | **Per Cake** 160 calories; 6g fat (of which 4g saturates); 6g carbohydrate; 0.2g salt | **18** |

**Freezing Tip**

**To freeze** Complete the recipe to the end of step 3. Open-freeze, then wrap and freeze.
**To use** Thaw for about 1 hour, then complete the recipe.

# Lavender and Honey Cupcakes

125g (4oz) unsalted butter, softened
125g (4oz) runny honey
2 medium eggs
125g (4oz) self-raising flour, sifted
1 tsp baking powder

**ICING AND DECORATION**
3 honey and lavender tea bags
2 tsp unsalted butter
250g (9oz) icing sugar, sifted
red and blue food colouring
purple sugar stars
edible silver dust (optional)

**1** Preheat the oven to 190°C (170°C fan oven), mark 5. Line a 12-hole muffin tin with 9 paper muffin cases.

**2** Using a hand-held electric whisk, whisk the butter and honey in a bowl, or beat with a wooden spoon, until combined. Gradually whisk in the eggs until just combined. Using a metal spoon, fold in the flour and baking powder until combined. Divide the mixture equally between the paper cases.

**3** Bake for 15–20 minutes until golden and risen. Cool in the tin for 5 minutes, then transfer to a wire rack and leave to cool completely.

**4** For the icing, infuse the tea bags in 50ml (2fl oz) boiling water in a small bowl for 5 minutes. Remove the tea bags and squeeze out the excess water into the bowl. Stir in the butter until melted. Put the icing sugar into a large bowl, add the infused tea mixture and stir to make a smooth icing. Add a few drops of red and blue food colouring until it is lilac in colour.

**5** Spoon a little icing on top of each cake, to flood the tops, then sprinkle with stars. Stand the cakes upright on the wire rack and leave for about 1 hour to set. Dust with edible dust, if you like, when set.

| Serves | EASY | | NUTRITIONAL INFORMATION |
|---|---|---|---|
| **9** | **Preparation Time** 35 minutes | **Cooking Time** 15–20 minutes, plus cooling and setting | **Per Cupcake** 316 calories; 13g fat (of which 8g saturates); 50g carbohydrate; 0.3g salt |

## Freezing Tip

**To freeze** Complete the recipe to the end of step 4.
Open-freeze, then wrap and freeze.
**To use** Thaw for about 1 hour, then complete the recipe.

# St Clements Cupcakes

1 small orange (about 200g/7oz)
175g (6oz) self-raising flour, sifted
100g (3½oz) caster sugar
100ml (3½fl oz) milk
1 medium egg, beaten
50g (2oz) unsalted butter, melted
1 tsp baking powder
grated zest of 1 large lemon

### ICING AND DECORATION

400g (14oz) royal icing sugar, sifted
juice and grated zest of 1 small orange
sugar star sprinkles
edible glitter (optional)

**1** Preheat the oven to 190°C (170°C fan oven), mark 5. Line a 12-hole muffin tin with 9 paper muffin cases.

**2** Grate the zest from the orange into a large bowl and set aside. Cut the top and bottom off the orange and stand it upright on a board. Using a serrated knife, cut away the pith in a downward motion. Roughly chop the orange flesh, discarding any pips. Put the chopped orange into a food processor and whiz until puréed.

**3** Transfer the orange purée into the bowl with the zest. Add the flour, caster sugar, milk, egg, melted butter, baking powder and lemon zest. Stir with a spatula until just combined. Divide the mixture equally between the paper cases.

**4** Bake for 15–18 minutes until golden and risen. Leave to cool in the tin for 5 minutes, then transfer to a wire rack to cool completely.

**5** For the topping, put the icing sugar, orange juice and zest into a bowl and whisk for 5 minutes or until soft peaks form. Spoon a little over the top of each cake to flood the top, then sprinkle with the stars. Stand the cakes upright on the wire rack and leave for about 1 hour to set. Dust with edible glitter, if you like, when set.

| EASY | | NUTRITIONAL INFORMATION | Serves |
|---|---|---|---|
| **Preparation Time**<br>40 minutes | **Cooking Time**<br>15–18 minutes, plus<br>cooling and setting | **Per Cupcake**<br>309 calorie; 1g fat (of which trace saturates);<br>76g carbohydrate; 0g salt | **9** |

### Freezing Tip

**To freeze** Complete the recipe to the end of step 2.
Open-freeze, then wrap and freeze.
**To use** Thaw for about 1 hour, then complete the recipe.

# Kitten Cupcakes

125g (4oz) unsalted butter, very soft
125g (4oz) caster sugar
grated zest of 1 lemon
2 medium eggs, beaten
125g (4oz) self-raising flour, sifted

### ICING AND DECORATION

175g (6oz) icing sugar
black and assorted writing icings
jelly diamonds and Smarties
black liquorice laces, cut into short lengths

**1** Preheat the oven to 190°C (170°C fan oven) mark 5.
Line a 12-hole bun tin with paper cases.

**2** Put the butter, caster sugar and lemon zest into a mixing bowl and, using a hand-held electric whisk, beat until pale and fluffy. Add the eggs, a little at a time, beating well after each addition. Fold in the flour. Divide the mixture between the paper cases. Bake for about 20 minutes or until golden and risen. Transfer to a wire rack to cool completely.

**3** Sift the icing sugar into a bowl. Stir in 1–2 tbsp warm water, a few drops at a time, until you have a smooth, spreadable icing. If necessary, slice the tops off the cooled buns to make them level. Cover the top of each cake with icing.

**4** Decorate the buns to make kittens' faces. Use black writing icing for the eyes, halve the jelly diamonds for the ears, press a Smartie in the centre for a nose, and use black writing icing to draw on a mouth. Use different coloured writing icing for the pupils and markings. Press on liquorice whiskers.

| Serves | EASY | | NUTRITIONAL INFORMATION |
|---|---|---|---|
| **12** | **Preparation Time** 25 minutes | **Cooking Time** 20 minutes, plus cooling | **Per Cupcake** 223 calories; 10g fat (of which 6g saturates); 34g carbohydrate; 0.2g salt |

## Freezing Tip

**To freeze** Complete the recipe to the end of step 3.
Open-freeze, then wrap and freeze.
**To use** Thaw for about 1 hour, then complete the recipe.

175g (6oz) unsalted butter, softened

175g (6oz) golden caster sugar

3 medium eggs

175g (6oz) self-raising flour, sifted

75g (3oz) dried cherries

2 tbsp milk

**ICING**

225g (8oz) golden icing sugar, sifted

3 tbsp lemon juice, strained

# Sour Cherry Cupcakes

**1** Preheat the oven to 190°C (170°C fan oven) mark 5. Line a 12-hole bun tin or muffin tin with paper muffin cases.

**2** Put the butter and caster sugar into a bowl and cream together until pale, light and fluffy. Beat in the eggs, one at a time, folding in 1 tbsp flour if the mixture looks like it is starting to curdle.

**3** Put 12 dried cherries to one side. Fold the remaining flour, the cherries and milk into the creamed mixture until evenly combined. Spoon the mixture into the paper cases and bake for 15–20 minutes until pale golden and risen. Transfer to a wire rack to cool completely.

**4** Put the icing sugar into a bowl and mix with the lemon juice to make a smooth dropping consistency. Spoon a little icing on to each cake and decorate each with a cherry, then stand the cakes upright on the wire rack and leave for about 1 hour to set.

| EASY | | NUTRITIONAL INFORMATION | Serves |
|---|---|---|---|
| **Preparation Time** 30 minutes | **Cooking Time** 15–20 minutes, plus cooling and setting | **Per Serving** 323 calories; 14g fat (of which 8g saturates); 50g carbohydrate; 0.4g salt | **12** |

## Freezing Tip

------------------------------------------------

**To freeze** Complete the recipe to the end of step 3.
Open-freeze, then wrap and freeze.
**To use** Thaw for about 1 hour, then complete the recipe.

## Cook's Tip

------------------------------------------------

To make the frosted flowers, whisk 1 medium egg white in
a clean bowl for 30 seconds or until frothy. Brush it over
12 violet petals and put on a wire rack. Lightly dust with
caster sugar and leave to dry.

# Vanilla and White Chocolate Cupcakes

125g (4oz) unsalted butter, at room temperature

125g (4oz) golden caster sugar

1 vanilla pod

2 medium eggs

125g (4oz) self-raising flour, sifted

1 tbsp vanilla extract

### TOPPING AND DECORATION

200g (7oz) white chocolate, broken into pieces

12 crystallised violets or frosted flowers (see Cook's Tip)

**1** Preheat the oven to 190°C (170°C fan oven) mark 5. Line a 12-hole bun tin or muffin tin with paper muffin cases.

**2** Put the butter and sugar into a bowl. Split the vanilla pod lengthways, scrape out the seeds and add to the bowl. Add the eggs, flour and vanilla extract and then, using a hand-held electric whisk, beat thoroughly until smooth and creamy. Spoon the mixture into the muffin cases.

**3** Bake for 15–20 minutes until pale golden, risen and springy to the touch. Leave in the tin for 2–3 minutes, then transfer to a wire rack to cool completely.

**4** Melt the chocolate in a heatproof bowl set over a pan of gently simmering water, making sure the base of the bowl doesn't touch the water. Stir until smooth and leave to cool slightly. Spoon the chocolate on to the cakes and top with a frosted flower. Stand the cakes upright on the wire rack and leave for about 1 hour to set

| Serves | EASY | | NUTRITIONAL INFORMATION |
|---|---|---|---|
| **12** | **Preparation Time** 25 minutes | **Cooking Time** 20–25 minutes, plus cooling and setting | **Per Cupcake** 270 calories; 15g fat (of which 9g saturates); 32g carbohydrate; 0.2g salt |

**Freezing Tip**

**To freeze** Complete the recipe to the end of step 3.
Open-freeze, then wrap and freeze.
**To use** Thaw for about 1 hour, then complete the recipe.

# Orange and Poppy Seed Cupcakes

175g (6oz) unsalted butter, softened
175g (6oz) caster sugar
3 medium eggs
175g (6oz) self-raising flour, sifted
grated zest and juice of 1 large orange
2 tbsp poppy seeds
1 tsp baking powder

### ICING AND DECORATION

125g (4oz) unsalted butter, softened
250g (9oz) icing sugar, sifted
1 tbsp orange flower water
12 orange jelly slices and orange edible glitter (optional)

**1** Preheat the oven to 190°C (170°C fan oven), mark 5. Line a 12-hole muffin tin with paper muffin cases.

**2** Using a hand-held electric whisk, whisk the butter and caster sugar in a bowl until pale and creamy, or beat with a wooden spoon. Gradually whisk in the eggs until just combined. Using a metal spoon, fold in the flour, orange zest and juice, poppy seeds and baking powder until combined. Divide the mixture equally between the paper cases.

**3** Bake for 20 minutes or until golden and risen. Cool in the tin for 5 minutes, then transfer to a wire rack and leave to cool completely.

**4** For the decoration, put the butter into a bowl and whisk until fluffy. Gradually add the icing sugar and orange flower water and whisk until light and fluffy.

**5** Insert a star nozzle into a piping bag, then fill the bag with the buttercream and pipe a swirl on to the top of each cake. Decorate each with an orange slice, and edible glitter, if you like.

| EASY | | NUTRITIONAL INFORMATION | Serves |
|---|---|---|---|
| **Preparation Time** 30 minutes | **Cooking Time** 20 minutes, plus cooling | **Per Cupcake** 408 calories; 24g fat (of which 14g saturates); 49g carbohydrate; 0.5g salt | **12** |

### Freezing Tip

**To freeze** Complete the recipe to the end of step 3. Open-freeze, then wrap and freeze.
**To use** Thaw for about 1 hour, then complete the recipe.

# Cookies and Cream Cupcakes

75g (3oz) mini Oreo cookies

175g (6oz) unsalted butter, softened

150g (5oz) caster sugar

3 medium eggs

175g (6oz) self-raising flour, sifted

½ tsp baking powder

3 tbsp milk

½ tsp vanilla extract

### ICING

75g (3oz) unsalted butter, softened

150g (5oz) icing sugar, sifted

2 tsp vanilla extract

1 tsp cocoa powder

**1** Preheat the oven to 200°C (180°C fan oven), mark 6. Line a 12-hole muffin tin with paper muffin cases. Reserve 12 mini cookies and roughly chop the remainder.

**2** Using a hand-held electric whisk, whisk the butter and caster sugar in a bowl (or beat with a wooden spoon) until pale and creamy. Gradually whisk in the eggs until just combined. Using a metal spoon, fold in the flour, baking powder, milk, vanilla extract and chopped cookies until combined. Divide the mixture equally between the paper cases.

**3** Bake for 15–20 minutes until golden and risen. Leave to cool in the tin for 5 minutes, then transfer to a wire rack to cool completely.

**4** For the decoration, put the butter into a bowl and whisk until fluffy. Gradually add the icing sugar and vanilla extract and whisk until light and fluffy. Using a small palette knife, spread the buttercream over the top of each cake. Sift a little cocoa powder on to the top of each cake and then decorate each with a reserved Oreo cookie.

| Serves 12 | EASY | | NUTRITIONAL INFORMATION |
|---|---|---|---|
| | **Preparation Time** 30 minutes | **Cooking Time** 15–20 minutes, plus cooling | **Per Cupcake** 357 calories; 21g fat (of which 13g saturates); 41g carbohydrate; 0.5g salt |

**Freezing Tip**

See opposite

**Try Something Different**

**Ginger and Orange Cupcakes:** Replace the lemon zest and juice with orange and add two pieces of drained and chopped preserved stem ginger. Omit the frosted flowers and make the icing with orange juice instead of lemon. Decorate with finely chopped stem ginger.

# Dainty Cupcakes

175g (6oz) unsalted butter, softened
175g (6oz) golden caster sugar
3 medium eggs
175g (6oz) self-raising flour, sifted
finely grated zest and juice of
1 lemon

**FROSTED FLOWERS**

1 medium egg white
6 edible flowers, such as violas
caster sugar to dust

**ICING**

225g (8oz) icing sugar, sifted
1 drop violet food colouring
2–3 tbsp lemon juice, strained

**1** Preheat the oven to 190°C (170°C fan oven) mark 5. Line a 12-hole bun tin or muffin tin with paper muffin cases.

**2** Put the butter and caster sugar into a bowl and cream together until pale, light and fluffy. Add the eggs, one at a time, and beat together, folding 1 tbsp flour into the mixture if it looks as if it is going to curdle. Fold in the flour, lemon zest and juice and mix well.

**3** Spoon the mixture into the cases and bake for 15–20 minutes until pale golden, risen and springy to the touch. Transfer to a wire rack to cool completely.

**4** To make the frosted flowers, whisk the egg white in a clean bowl for 30 seconds or until frothy. Brush over the flower petals and put on a wire rack resting on a piece of greaseproof paper. Dust heavily with caster sugar, then leave the flowers to dry.

**5** To make the icing, put the icing sugar into a bowl with the food colouring. Mix in the lemon juice to make a smooth dropping consistency. Spoon the icing on to the cakes, then decorate with the frosted flowers. Stand the cakes upright on the wire rack and leave for about 1 hour to set.

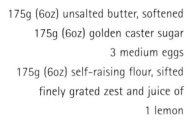

| EASY | | NUTRITIONAL INFORMATION | Serves |
|---|---|---|---|
| **Preparation Time** 15 minutes, plus drying | **Cooking Time** 15–20 minutes, plus cooling and setting | **Per Cupcake** 306 calories; 14g fat (of which 8g saturates); 46g carbohydrate; 0.4g salt | **12** |

## Freezing Tip

**To freeze** Complete the recipe to the end of step 3.
Open-freeze, then wrap and freeze.
**To use** Thaw for about 1 hour, then complete the recipe.

275g (10oz) plain flour, sifted

1 tbsp baking powder

100g (3½oz) caster sugar

grated zest of 1 lime

50g (2oz) desiccated coconut

2 medium eggs

100ml (3½fl oz) sunflower oil

225g (8oz) natural yogurt

50ml (2fl oz) milk

# Coconut and Lime Cupcakes

### TOPPING

150g (5oz) icing sugar, sifted

juice of 1 lime

50g (2oz) desiccated coconut

**1** Preheat the oven to 200°C (180°C fan oven), mark 6.
Line a 12-hole muffin tin with paper muffin cases.

**2** Put the flour, baking powder, caster sugar, lime zest
and coconut into a large bowl. Put the eggs, oil,
yogurt and milk into a jug and lightly beat together
until combined. Pour the yogurt mixture into the
flour and stir with a spatula until just combined.
Divide the mixture equally between the paper cases.

**3** Bake for 18–20 minutes until lightly golden and
risen. Cool in the tin for 5 minutes, then transfer to
a wire rack and leave to cool completely.

**4** For the decoration, mix the icing sugar with the lime
juice and 1–2 tsp boiling water, enough to make a
thick, smooth icing. Put the coconut into a shallow
bowl. Dip each cake top into the icing until coated,
allowing the excess to drip off, then carefully dip into
the coconut until coated. Stand the cakes upright on
the wire rack and leave for about 1 hour to set.

| Serves | EASY | | NUTRITIONAL INFORMATION |
|---|---|---|---|
| **12** | **Preparation Time** 30 minutes | **Cooking Time** 18–20 minutes, plus cooling and setting | **Per Cupcake** 291 calories; 13g fat (of which 6g saturates); 42g carbohydrate; 0.1g salt |

## Freezing Tip

**To freeze** Complete the recipe to the end of step 3. Open-freeze, then wrap and freeze.
**To use** Thaw for about 1 hour, then complete the recipe.

# Toast and Marmalade Cupcakes

150g (5oz) low-fat olive oil spread
200g (7oz) wholemeal self-raising flour, sifted
150g (5oz) light soft brown sugar
3 medium eggs
50g (2oz) marmalade
100ml (3¹/₂fl oz) milk
grated zest of 1 orange
50g (2oz) fresh wholemeal breadcrumbs

### ICING AND DECORATION
125g (4oz) marmalade
300g (11oz) icing sugar, sifted

**1** Preheat the oven to 180°C (160°C fan oven), mark 4. Line a 12-hole muffin tin with paper muffin cases.

**2** Put the low-fat spread, flour, brown sugar, eggs, marmalade, milk, orange zest and breadcrumbs into a large bowl. Using a hand-held electric whisk, whisk together until pale and creamy. Divide the mixture equally between the paper cases.

**3** Bake for 20–25 minutes until golden and risen. Cool in the tin for 5 minutes, then transfer to a wire rack and leave to cool completely.

**4** For the icing, pass the marmalade through a sieve into a bowl to remove the rind. Reserve the rind. Mix the icing sugar with the sieved marmalade in the bowl until it forms a smooth icing. Spoon a little icing on to each cake to flood the top, then scatter on the reserved rind. Stand the cakes upright on the wire rack and leave for about 1 hour to set.

| EASY | | NUTRITIONAL INFORMATION | Serves |
|---|---|---|---|
| **Preparation Time**<br>30 minutes | **Cooking Time**<br>20–25 minutes, plus<br>cooling and setting | **Per Cupcake**<br>336 calories; 10g fat (of which 2g saturates);<br>57g carbohydrate; 1.5g salt | **12** |

# Pavlova Cupcakes

125g (4oz) unsalted butter, softened
100g (3½oz) caster sugar
2 medium eggs
150g (5oz) self-raising flour, sifted
1 tbsp milk
grated zest of 1 lemon
50g (2oz) small fresh blueberries
12 fresh raspberries

## FROSTING

1 medium egg white
175g (6oz) caster sugar
pinch of cream of tartar

**1** Preheat the oven to 190°C (170°C fan oven), mark 5. Line a 12-hole muffin tin with paper cake cases.

**2** Using a hand-held electric whisk, whisk the butter and sugar in a bowl, or beat with a wooden spoon, until pale and creamy. Gradually whisk in the eggs until just combined. Using a metal spoon, fold in the flour, milk, lemon zest and blueberries until combined. Divide the mixture equally between the paper cases and press 1 raspberry into the centre of each cake.

**3** Bake for 15 minutes or until golden and risen. Cool in the tin for 5 minutes, then transfer to a wire rack and leave to cool completely.

**4** For the frosting, put all the ingredients into a heatproof bowl with 2 tbsp water and whisk lightly, using a hand-held electric whisk. Put the bowl over a pan of simmering water and whisk continuously for about 7 minutes until the mixture thickens sufficiently to stand in peaks.

**5** Insert a star nozzle into a piping bag, then fill the bag with the frosting and pipe a swirl on to the top of each cake. Stand the cakes upright on the wire rack and leave for about 1 hour to set.

## Freezing Tip

------------------------------------------------

**To freeze** Complete the recipe to the end of step 3. Open-freeze, then wrap and freeze.
**To use** Thaw for about 1 hour, then complete the recipe.

| Serves | EASY | | NUTRITIONAL INFORMATION |
|---|---|---|---|
| **12** | **Preparation Time** 30 minutes | **Cooking Time** 25 minutes, plus cooling and setting | **Per Cupcake** 226 calories; 10g fat (of which 6g saturates); 34g carbohydrate; 0.2g salt |

**Freezing Tip**

**To freeze** Complete the recipe to the end of step 3. Open-freeze, then wrap and freeze.
**To use** Thaw for about 1 hour, then complete the recipe.

# Cherry Bakewell Cupcakes

175g (6oz) unsalted butter, softened

175g (6oz) caster sugar

3 medium eggs

150g (5oz) self-raising flour, sifted

1 tsp baking powder

75g (3oz) ground almonds

1 tsp almond extract

75g (3oz) glacé cherries, finely chopped

### ICING AND DECORATION

1 tbsp custard powder

100ml (3½fl oz) milk

50g (2oz) unsalted butter, softened

250g (9oz) icing sugar, sifted

red sugar sprinkles

**1** Preheat the oven to 190°C (170°C fan oven), mark 5. Line a 12-hole muffin tin with paper muffin cases.

**2** Using a hand-held electric whisk, whisk the butter and caster sugar in a bowl, or beat with a wooden spoon, until pale and creamy. Gradually whisk in the eggs until just combined. Using a metal spoon, fold in the flour, baking powder, ground almonds, almond extract and cherries until combined. Divide the mixture equally between the paper cases.

**3** Bake for 20 minutes or until golden and risen. Cool in the tin for 5 minutes, then transfer to a wire rack and leave to cool completely.

**4** For the topping, put the custard powder into a jug and add a little of the milk to make a smooth paste. Put the remaining milk into a saucepan and bring just to the boil. Pour the hot milk on to the custard paste and stir. Return to the milk pan and heat gently for 1–2 minutes until it thickens. Remove from the heat, cover with dampened greaseproof paper to prevent a skin forming and cool completely.

**5** Put the custard in a bowl. Using a hand-held electric whisk, whisk in the butter. Chill for 30 minutes.

**6** Gradually whisk the icing sugar into the chilled custard mixture until you have a smooth, thick icing. Using a small palette knife, spread a little custard cream over the top of each cake, then decorate with sugar sprinkles. Stand the cakes upright on the wire rack and leave for about 1 hour to set.

| Serves | EASY | | NUTRITIONAL INFORMATION |
|---|---|---|---|
| **12** | **Preparation Time**<br>30 minutes | **Cooking Time**<br>25 minutes, plus<br>cooling and setting | **Per Cupcake**<br>405 calories; 21g fat (of which 11g saturates);<br>53g carbohydrate; 0.4g salt |

### Freezing Tip

**To freeze** Complete the recipe to the end of step 4.
Open-freeze, then wrap and freeze.
**To use** Thaw for about 1 hour, then complete the recipe.

# Sticky Gingerbread Cupcakes

175g (6oz) self-raising flour
75g (3oz) unsalted butter, chilled and cut into cubes
¼ tsp bicarbonate of soda
2 tsp ground ginger
25g (1oz) stem ginger in syrup, finely chopped, plus 3 tbsp syrup from the jar
50g (2oz) dark muscovado sugar
50g (2oz) golden syrup
50g (2oz) treacle
juice of 1 orange
2 medium eggs, beaten

### ICING AND DECORATION

100g (3½oz) unsalted butter, softened
200g (7oz) icing sugar, sifted
3 tbsp syrup from the stem ginger jar
1 tsp ground ginger
ready-made sugar flowers (optional)

**1** Preheat the oven to 190°C (170°C fan oven), mark 5. Line a 12-hole muffin tin with 9 paper muffin cases.

**2** Put the flour into a large bowl and, using your fingertips, rub in the butter until it resembles breadcrumbs. Stir in the bicarbonate of soda, ground ginger and stem ginger and set aside. Put the muscovado sugar, syrup, treacle and orange juice into a small saucepan and heat gently until the sugar dissolves. Leave to cool for 5 minutes.

**3** Mix the eggs and warm sugar mixture into the flour mixture and stir with a spatula until just combined. Divide equally between the paper cases.

**4** Bake for 20 minutes or until golden and risen. Remove from the oven and drizzle each cake with 1 tsp ginger syrup. Leave to cool in the tin for 5 minutes, then transfer to a wire rack to cool completely.

**5** For the buttercream topping, put the butter into a bowl and whisk until fluffy. Add the icing sugar, ginger syrup and ground ginger. Whisk until light and fluffy. Using a small palette knife, spread a little buttercream over the top of each cake. Decorate with sugar flowers, if you like

| EASY | | NUTRITIONAL INFORMATION | Serves |
|---|---|---|---|
| **Preparation Time** 35 minutes | **Cooking Time** 25 minutes, plus cooling | **Per Cupcake** 386 calories; 17g fat (of which 11g saturates); 58g carbohydrate; 0.5g salt | **9** |

## Freezing Tip

**To freeze** Complete the recipe. Open-freeze, then wrap and freeze.
**To use** Thaw for about 1 hour, then serve.

320g (11½oz) eating apples, cored (about 2)

juice of 1 lemon

200g (7oz) self-raising flour, sifted

1 tsp baking powder

1 tsp ground cinnamon

125g (4oz) light soft brown sugar

2 medium eggs

100g (3½oz) unsalted butter, melted

# Apple Crumble Cupcakes

### CRUMBLE TOPPING

50g (2oz) plain flour

25g (1oz) unsalted butter, chilled and cut into cubes

15g (½oz) light soft brown sugar

**1** Preheat the oven to 180°C (160°C fan oven), mark 4. Line a 12-hole muffin tin with paper muffin cases.

**2** Make the crumble. Put the flour into a bowl and, using your fingertips, rub in the butter until it resembles coarse breadcrumbs. Stir in the sugar and set aside.

**3** Coarsely grate the apples into a large bowl and mix in the lemon juice. Add the flour, baking powder, cinnamon and sugar. Put the eggs and melted butter into a jug and lightly beat together, then pour into the flour mixture. Stir with a spatula until just combined. Divide the mixture equally between the paper cases, then sprinkle the crumble equally over the top of each cake.

**4** Bake for 25 minutes or until lightly golden and risen. Leave to cool in the tin for 5 minutes, then transfer to a wire rack to cool completely.

| Serves | EASY | | NUTRITIONAL INFORMATION |
|---|---|---|---|
| | **Preparation Time** | **Cooking Time** | **Per Cupcake** |
| 12 | 20 minutes | 25 minutes, plus cooling | 215 calories; 10g fat (of which 6g saturates); 31g carbohydrate; 0.2g salt |

## Freezing Tip

**To freeze** Complete the recipe to the end of step 3.
Open-freeze, then wrap and freeze.
**To use** Thaw for about 1 hour, then complete the recipe.

# Coffee Walnut Whip Cupcakes

100g (3½oz) walnuts
175g (6oz) unsalted butter, softened
150g (5oz) self-raising flour, sifted
175g (6oz) light soft brown sugar
3 medium eggs
1 tsp baking powder
50ml (2fl oz) milk

### ICING AND DECORATION

1 tbsp instant coffee granules
50g (2oz) unsalted butter, softened
200g (7oz) icing sugar, sifted
50g (2oz) walnuts, finely chopped

**1** Preheat the oven to 190°C (170°C fan oven), mark 5. Line a 12-hole muffin tin with paper muffin cases.

**2** Whiz the walnuts in a food processor until finely ground. Transfer to a large bowl. Add the butter, flour, brown sugar, eggs, baking powder and milk to the ground walnuts. Using a hand-held electric whisk, whisk together until pale and creamy. Divide the mixture equally between the paper cases.

**3** Bake for 20–25 minutes until golden and risen. Leave to cool in the tin for 5 minutes, then transfer to a wire rack to cool completely.

**4** For the icing, put 2 tbsp boiling water into a small bowl, add the coffee and stir to dissolve. Put the butter, half the icing sugar and the coffee mixture into a bowl and whisk until combined. Chill for 30 minutes.

**5** Remove the buttercream from the fridge and gradually whisk in the remaining icing sugar until smooth and fluffy. Using a small palette knife, spread a little buttercream over the top of each cake. Put the chopped walnuts into a shallow bowl and lightly dip the top of each cake into the walnuts.

| EASY | | NUTRITIONAL INFORMATION | Serves |
|---|---|---|---|
| **Preparation Time** 30 minutes | **Cooking Time** 20–25 minutes, plus cooling and chilling | **Per Cupcake** 409 calories; 26g fat (of which 11g saturates); 43g carbohydrate; 0.5g salt | **12** |

# Raspberry Ripple Cupcakes

50g (2oz) seedless raspberry jam

50g (2oz) fresh raspberries

125g (4oz) unsalted butter, softened

100g (3½oz) caster sugar

2 medium eggs

1 tbsp milk

150g (5oz) self-raising flour, sifted

**TOPPING AND DECORATION**

150g (5oz) fresh raspberries

300ml (½ pint) whipping cream

50g (2oz) icing sugar, sifted

**1** Preheat the oven to 190°C (170°C fan oven), mark 5. Line a 12-hole muffin tin with 9 paper muffin cases.

**2** Mix the raspberry jam with the 50g (2oz) raspberries, lightly crushing the raspberries. Set aside.

**3** Using a hand-held electric whisk, whisk the butter and caster sugar in a bowl, or beat with a wooden spoon, until pale and creamy. Gradually whisk in the eggs and milk until just combined. Using a metal spoon, fold in the flour until just combined, then carefully fold in the raspberry jam mixture until just marbled, being careful not to overmix. Divide the mixture equally between the paper cases.

**4** Bake for 20 minutes or until golden and risen. Cool in the tin for 5 minutes, then transfer to a wire rack and leave to cool completely.

**5** For the decoration, reserve 9 raspberries. Mash the remaining raspberries in a bowl with a fork. Pass through a sieve into a bowl to remove the seeds. Using a hand-held electric whisk, whisk the cream and icing sugar together until stiff peaks form. Mix the raspberry purée into the cream until combined.

**6** Insert a star nozzle into a piping bag, then fill the bag with the cream and pipe a swirl on to the top of each cake. Decorate each with a raspberry.

## Freezing Tip

**To freeze** Complete the recipe to the end of step 4. Open-freeze, then wrap and freeze.

**To use** Thaw for about 1 hour, then complete the recipe.

| EASY | | NUTRITIONAL INFORMATION | Serves |
|---|---|---|---|
| **Preparation Time**<br>30 minutes | **Cooking Time**<br>20 minutes,<br>plus cooling | **Per Cupcake**<br>385 calories; 26g fat (of which 16g saturates);<br>36g carbohydrate; 0.5g salt | **9** |

# The Ultimate Carrot Cupcakes

150g (5oz) carrots, peeled
50g (2oz) raisins
175g (6oz) self-raising flour, sifted
½ tsp bicarbonate of soda
150g (5oz) light soft brown sugar
grated zest of 1 orange
½ tsp ground mixed spice
3 medium eggs
100ml (3½fl oz) sunflower oil
75ml (2½fl oz) buttermilk

**ICING AND DECORATION**
50g (2oz) icing sugar, sifted
250g (9oz) mascarpone cheese
100g (3½oz) quark cheese
juice of ½ orange
red, yellow and green ready-made fondant icing (optional)

**1** Preheat the oven to 190°C (170°C fan oven), mark 5. Line a 12-hole muffin tin with paper muffin cases.

**2** Coarsely grate the carrots and put into a large bowl. Add the raisins, flour, bicarbonate of soda, brown sugar, orange zest and mixed spice. Put the eggs, oil and buttermilk into a jug and lightly beat together until combined. Pour the egg mixture into the flour and stir with a spatula until just combined. Divide the mixture equally between the paper cases.

**3** Bake for 20 minutes or until lightly golden and risen. Cool in the tin for 5 minutes, then transfer to a wire rack and leave to cool completely.

**4** For the topping, mix the icing sugar with the mascarpone, quark and orange juice to a smooth icing. Using a small palette knife, spread a little of the icing over each cake. Use the coloured fondant to make small carrots, if you like, and decorate the cakes with them.

| Serves | EASY | | NUTRITIONAL INFORMATION |
|---|---|---|---|
| **12** | **Preparation Time** 30 minutes | **Cooking Time** 20 minutes, plus cooling | **Per Cupcake** 255 calories; 12g fat (of which 4g saturates); 34g carbohydrate; 0.3g salt |

## Freezing Tip

**To freeze** Complete the recipe to the end of step 3.
Open-freeze, then wrap and freeze.
**To use** Thaw for about 1 hour, then complete the recipe.

125g (4oz) unsalted butter, softened

100g (3½oz) caster sugar

2 medium eggs

125g (4oz) self-raising flour, sifted

½ tsp baking powder

1 x 51g bar Turkish Delight, finely chopped

1 tbsp rosewater

### ICING AND DECORATION

75g (3oz) unsalted butter, softened

250g (9oz) icing sugar, sifted

2 tbsp rosewater

pink and white heart-shaped sugar sprinkles

about 12 Loveheart sweets (optional)

# Be Mine Cupcakes

**1** Preheat the oven to 190°C (170°C fan oven), mark 5. Line a 12-hole muffin tin with paper cake cases.

**2** Using a hand-held electric whisk, whisk the butter and caster sugar in a bowl, or beat with a wooden spoon, until pale and creamy. Gradually whisk in the eggs until just combined. Using a metal spoon, fold in the flour, baking powder, Turkish Delight and rosewater until combined. Divide the mixture equally between the paper cases.

**3** Bake for 15 minutes or until golden and risen. Leave to cool in the tin for 5 minutes, then transfer to a wire rack to cool completely.

**4** For the topping, put the butter into a bowl and whisk until fluffy. Add the icing sugar and rosewater and whisk until light and fluffy. Using a small palette knife, spread a little buttercream over the top of each cake. Decorate with sugar hearts, then top each with a Loveheart, if you like.

| EASY | | NUTRITIONAL INFORMATION | Serves |
|---|---|---|---|
| **Preparation Time** 30 minutes | **Cooking Time** 15 minutes, plus cooling | **Per Cupcake** 289 calories; 15g fat (of which 9g saturates); 40g carbohydrate; 0.3g salt | **12** |

**Freezing Tip**

-------------------------------------------------

**To freeze** Complete the recipe to the end of step 3.
Open-freeze, then wrap and freeze.
**To use** Thaw for about 1 hour, then complete the recipe.

# Rocky Road Cupcakes

100g (3¹/₂oz) unsalted butter, softened
125g (4oz) caster sugar
2 medium eggs
150g (5oz) self-raising flour, sifted
25g (1oz) glacé cherries, diced
25g (1oz) milk chocolate chips
25g (1oz) pinenuts

**TOPPING**

100g (3¹/₂oz) milk chocolate
50ml (2fl oz) double cream
25g (1oz) mini marshmallows
25g (1oz) glacé cherries, finely chopped
1 x 37g bag Maltesers

**1** Preheat the oven to 190°C (170°C fan oven), mark 5. Line a 12-hole muffin tin with 9 paper muffin cases.

**2** Using a hand-held electric whisk, whisk the butter and sugar in a bowl, or beat with a wooden spoon, until pale and creamy. Gradually whisk in the eggs until just combined. Using a metal spoon, fold in the flour, cherries, chocolate chips and pinenuts until combined. Divide the mixture equally between the paper cases.

**3** Bake for 15–20 minutes until golden and risen. Leave to cool in the tin for 5 minutes, then transfer to a wire rack to cool completely.

**4** For the topping, break the chocolate into pieces, then put into a heatproof bowl with the cream. Set over a pan of gently simmering water, making sure the base of the bowl doesn't touch the water. Heat until melted, stirring occasionally until smooth.

**5** Remove from the heat and, using a small palette knife, spread a little over the top of each cake. Decorate each with marshmallows, cherries and Maltesers. Stand the cakes upright on the wire rack and leave for about 1 hour to set.

| Serves | EASY | | NUTRITIONAL INFORMATION |
| --- | --- | --- | --- |
| **9** | **Preparation Time** 30 minutes | **Cooking Time** 25–30 minutes, plus cooling and setting | **Per Cupcake** 360 calories; 20g fat (of which 11g saturates); 45g carbohydrate; 0.5g salt |

**Freezing Tip**

**To freeze** Complete the recipe to the end of step 4.
Open-freeze, then wrap and freeze.
**To use** Thaw for about 1 hour, then complete the recipe.

# Peanut Butter Cupcakes

75g (3oz) unsalted peanuts or cashew nuts, toasted

100g (3½oz) unsalted butter, softened

50g (2oz) light soft brown sugar

50g (2oz) dark muscovado sugar

3 medium eggs

175g (6oz) self-raising flour, sifted

½ tsp baking powder

## TOPPING

100ml (3½fl oz) milk

50g (2oz) cocoa powder

300g (11oz) icing sugar

100g (3½oz) peanut butter

chocolate sprinkles or vermicelli

**1** Preheat the oven to 190°C (170°C fan oven), mark 5. Line a 12-hole muffin tin with paper muffin cases.

**2** Whiz the peanuts or cashews in a food processor until finely ground. Set aside.

**3** Using a hand-held electric whisk, whisk the butter with the light brown and muscovado sugars, or beat with a wooden spoon, until pale and creamy. Gradually whisk in the eggs until just combined. Using a metal spoon, fold in the flour, baking powder and finely ground nuts until combined. Divide the mixture equally between the paper cases.

**4** Bake for 20 minutes or until golden and risen. Leave to cool in the tin for 5 minutes, then transfer to a wire rack to cool completely.

**5** For the decoration, warm the milk in a small saucepan. Sift the cocoa and icing sugar into a bowl, then gradually stir in the warm milk until it forms a smooth icing.

**6** Put a small spoonful of peanut butter on the top of each cake and then spoon the chocolate icing on to cover the peanut butter and to coat the top of the cupcake. Decorate with sprinkles or vermicelli. Stand the cakes upright on the wire rack and leave for about 1 hour to set.

| **EASY** | | **NUTRITIONAL INFORMATION** | **Serves** |
|---|---|---|---|
| **Preparation Time** 30 minutes | **Cooking Time** 25 minutes, plus cooling and setting | **Per Cupcake** 363 calories; 17g fat (of which 7g saturates); 49g carbohydrate; 0.5g salt | **12** |

## Freezing Tip

**To freeze** Complete the recipe to the end of step 3.
Open-freeze, then wrap and freeze.
**To use** Thaw for about 1 hour, then complete the recipe.

50g (2oz) unsalted butter, very soft

50g (2oz) caster sugar

1 medium egg, beaten

50g (2oz) self-raising flour

¼ tsp baking powder

1 ripe banana, peeled and mashed

### ICING AND DECORATION

125g (4oz) icing sugar, sifted

about 1 tbsp orange juice

red glacé cherries or round red jelly sweets

# Red Nose Buns

**1** Preheat the oven to 190°C (170°C fan oven) mark 5. Arrange about 36 petits fours cases on baking sheets.

**2** Put the butter, caster sugar, egg, flour and baking powder into a food processor and whiz until smooth and well mixed. Add the banana and whiz for 1 minute. Put a teaspoonful of the mixture into each paper case.

**3** Bake for 12–15 minutes until golden. Transfer to a wire rack to cool completely.

**4** For the icing, mix the icing sugar with the orange juice until smooth and just thick enough to coat the back of a spoon. Top each bun with a small blob of icing and stick half a cherry or a sweet on each one. Stand the cakes upright on the wire rack and leave for about 1 hour to set.

| Serves 36 | EASY | | NUTRITIONAL INFORMATION |
|---|---|---|---|
| | **Preparation Time** 20 minutes | **Cooking Time** 12–15 minutes, plus cooling and setting | **Per Bun** 39 calories; 1g fat (of which 1g saturates); 7g carbohydrate; 0g salt |

## Freezing Tip

**To freeze** Complete the recipe to the end of step 3.
Open-freeze, then wrap and freeze.
**To use** Thaw for about 1 hour, then complete the recipe.

# Polka Dot Cupcakes

250g (9oz) plain flour, sifted
1 tbsp baking powder
100g (3½oz) caster sugar
1 tbsp vanilla extract
2 medium eggs
125ml (4fl oz) sunflower oil
175g (6oz) natural yogurt

**ICING AND DECORATION**

50g (2oz) unsalted butter, softened
175g (6oz) icing sugar, sifted
25g (1oz) cocoa powder, sifted
mini Smarties or chocolate beans

**1** Preheat the oven to 190°C (170°C fan oven), mark 5. Line a 12-hole muffin tin with paper muffin cases.

**2** Put the flour, baking powder and caster sugar into a large bowl. Put the vanilla extract, eggs, oil and yogurt into a jug and lightly beat together until combined. Pour into the flour mixture and stir with a spatula until just combined. Divide the mixture equally between the paper cases.

**3** Bake for 20 minutes or until lightly golden and risen. Leave to cool in the tin for 5 minutes, then transfer to a wire rack to cool completely.

**4** For the topping, put the butter into a bowl and whisk until fluffy. Gradually add the icing sugar until combined. Add the cocoa powder and 2 tbsp boiling water and whisk until light and fluffy. Using a small palette knife, spread a little buttercream over the top of each cake. Decorate with mini Smarties or chocolate beans.

| EASY | | NUTRITIONAL INFORMATION | Serves |
|---|---|---|---|
| **Preparation Time** 30 minutes | **Cooking Time** 20 minutes, plus cooling | **Per Cupcake** 283 calories; 12g fat (of which 4g saturates); 42g carbohydrate; 0.2g salt | **12** |

# Mango and Passion Fruit Cupcakes

4 ripe passion fruit

about 75ml (2½fl oz) orange juice

150g (5oz) unsalted butter, softened

250g (9oz) plain flour, sifted

175g (6oz) caster sugar

3 medium eggs

1 tbsp baking powder

75g (3oz) ready-to-eat dried mango, finely chopped

### ICING AND DECORATION

100g (3½oz) cream cheese

25g (1oz) unsalted butter, softened

200g (7oz) icing sugar, sifted

1 large, ripe passion fruit

white sugar sprinkles

**1** Preheat the oven to 180°C (160°C fan oven), mark 4. Line a 12–hole muffin tin with paper muffin cases.

**2** Cut the passion fruit in half and pass the seeds and juice through a sieve into a jug. Discard the seeds. You need 150ml (¼ pint) liquid, so use the orange juice to top up the passion fruit juice.

**3** Put the butter, flour, caster sugar, eggs, baking powder and passion fruit and orange juice into a large bowl. Using a hand-held electric whisk, whisk together, or beat with a wooden spoon, until pale and creamy. Add the chopped mango and fold through until combined. Divide the mixture equally between the paper cases.

**4** Bake for 25 minutes or until golden and risen. Leave to cool in the tin for 5 minutes, then transfer to a wire rack to cool completely.

**5** For the topping, whisk together the cream cheese and butter until fluffy. Gradually add the icing sugar until combined. Cut the passion fruit in half and pass the seeds and juice through a sieve into the icing. Discard the seeds. Stir to combine, then, using a small palette knife, spread a little over the top of each cake. Scatter on the sugar sprinkles.

| Serves | EASY | | NUTRITIONAL INFORMATION |
|---|---|---|---|
| **12** | **Preparation Time**<br>30 minutes | **Cooking Time**<br>25 minutes,<br>plus cooling | **Per Cupcake**<br>374 calories; 18g fat (of which 11g saturates);<br>52g carbohydrate; 0.4g salt |

## Freezing Tip

**To freeze** Complete the recipe to the end of step 4.
Open-freeze, then wrap and freeze.
**To use** Thaw for about 1 hour, then complete the recipe.

# Gluten-free Pistachio and Polenta Cupcakes

150g (5oz) shelled pistachio nuts
175g (6oz) unsalted butter, softened
175g (6oz) caster sugar
3 medium eggs
200g (7oz) fine polenta
½ tsp baking powder
150g (5oz) ground almonds
grated zest of 2 lemons
2 tbsp milk

### ICING

75g (3oz) unsalted butter, softened
300g (11oz) icing sugar, sifted
juice of 2 lemons

**1** Preheat the oven to 180°C (160°C fan oven), mark 4. Line a 12-hole muffin tin with paper muffin cases.

**2** Whiz the pistachios in a food processor until really finely chopped.

**3** Using a hand-held electric whisk, whisk the butter and caster sugar in a bowl, or beat with a wooden spoon, until pale and creamy. Gradually whisk in the eggs until just combined. Using a metal spoon, fold in the polenta, baking powder, ground almonds, lemon zest, milk and 100g (3½oz) ground pistachios until combined. Divide the mixture equally between the paper cases.

**4** Bake for 25 minutes or until golden and risen. Cool in the tin for 5 minutes, then transfer to a wire rack and leave to cool completely.

**5** For the icing, put the butter into a bowl and whisk until fluffy. Gradually whisk in half the icing sugar, then add the lemon juice and the remaining icing sugar, whisking until light and fluffy. Using a small palette knife, spread a little of the buttercream over the top of each cake, then sprinkle each with a little of the remaining chopped pistachios.

| EASY | | NUTRITIONAL INFORMATION | Serves |
|---|---|---|---|
| **Preparation Time** 35 minutes | **Cooking Time** 25 minutes, plus cooling | **Per Cupcake** 542 calories; 33g fat (of which 13g saturates); 56g carbohydrate; 0.6g salt | **12** |

**Freezing Tip**

------------------------------------------------

**To freeze** Complete the recipe to the end of step 3.
Open-freeze, then wrap and freeze.
**To use** Thaw for about 1 hour, then complete the recipe.

# Mallow Madness Cupcakes

3 medium eggs
175g (6oz) self-raising flour, sifted
150g (5oz) caster sugar
175ml (6fl oz) sunflower oil
½ tsp baking powder
50g (2oz) white chocolate chips

### TOPPING AND DECORATION

125g (4oz) pink and white marshmallows
1 medium egg white
150g (5oz) caster sugar
pinch of cream of tartar
pink sugar sprinkles

**1** Preheat the oven to 190°C (170°C fan oven), mark 5. Line a 12-hole muffin tin with paper muffin cases.

**2** Put the eggs, flour, sugar, oil and baking powder into a large bowl and, using a hand-held electric whisk, whisk until just combined. Add the chocolate chips and fold through. Divide between the paper cases.

**3** Bake for 20–25 minutes until lightly golden and risen. Leave to cool in the tin for 5 minutes, then transfer to a wire rack to cool completely.

**4** For the decoration, reserve 6 white marshmallows. Put the remaining marshmallows, the egg white, sugar and a pinch of cream of tartar into a heatproof bowl and whisk lightly using a hand-held electric whisk. Put the bowl over a pan of simmering water and whisk continuously, for about 7 minutes or until the marshmallows have melted and the mixture thickens sufficiently to stand in peaks.

**5** Cut the reserved marshmallows in half. Spread a little of the icing over each cake. Scatter with sprinkles and top each with a marshmallow half. Stand the cakes on the wire rack and leave for about 1 hour to set.

| Serves 12 | EASY | | NUTRITIONAL INFORMATION |
|---|---|---|---|
| | **Preparation Time** 30 minutes | **Cooking Time** 30–35 minutes, plus cooling and setting | **Per Cupcake** 317 calories; 13g fat (of which 2g saturates); 49g carbohydrate; 0.1g salt |

## Freezing Tip

**To freeze** Complete the recipe to the end of step 3.
Open-freeze, then wrap and freeze.
**To use** Thaw for about 1 hour, then complete the recipe.

175g (6oz) unsalted butter, softened

100g (3½oz) caster sugar

3 medium eggs

75g (3oz) apricot jam

150g (5oz) self-raising flour, sifted

75g (3oz) oatbran

½ tsp baking powder

# Breakfast Cupcakes

**ICING AND DECORATION**

225g (8oz) icing sugar

1–2 tbsp orange juice

75g (3oz) mixed berry granola

**1** Preheat the oven to 190°C (170°C fan oven), mark 5. Line a 12-hole muffin tin with paper muffin cases.

**2** Using a hand-held electric whisk, whisk the butter and caster sugar in a bowl, or beat with a wooden spoon, until pale and creamy. Gradually whisk in the eggs until just combined. Using a metal spoon, fold in the apricot jam, flour, oatbran and baking powder until combined. Divide the mixture equally between the paper cases.

**3** Bake for 20 minutes or until golden and risen. Leave to cool in the tin for 5 minutes, then transfer to a wire rack to cool completely.

**4** For the icing, sift the icing sugar into a bowl, then add enough orange juice to achieve a smooth, thick icing. Spoon a little on top of each cake, then sprinkle with the granola. Stand the cakes upright on the wire rack and leave for about 1 hour to set.

| EASY | | NUTRITIONAL INFORMATION | Serves |
|---|---|---|---|
| **Preparation Time** 30 minutes | **Cooking Time** 20 minutes, plus cooling and setting | **Per Cupcake** 327 calories; 14g fat (of which 8g saturates); 48g carbohydrate; 0.3g salt | **12** |

# Mini Green Tea Cupcakes

100ml (3¹/₂fl oz) milk

2 tsp loose green tea leaves

100g (3¹/₂oz) unsalted butter, softened

125g (4oz) caster sugar

2 medium eggs

150g (5oz) self-raising flour, sifted

¹/₄ tsp baking powder

**ICING AND DECORATION**

3 tsp loose green tea leaves

75g (3oz) unsalted butter, softened

250g (9oz) icing sugar, sifted

ready-made sugar flowers

**1** Preheat the oven to 190°C (170°C fan oven), mark 5. Line a 12-hole muffin tin with paper cake or cases.

**2** Put the milk into a small saucepan and bring to the boil. Add the green tea leaves and leave to infuse for 30 minutes.

**3** Using a hand-held electric whisk, whisk the butter and caster sugar in a bowl, or beat with a wooden spoon, until pale and creamy. Gradually whisk in the eggs until just combined. Pass the green tea milk through a sieve into the bowl, then discard the tea. Using a metal spoon, fold in the flour and baking powder until combined. Divide the mixture equally between the paper cases.

**4** Bake for 18–20 minutes until golden and risen. Cool in the tin for 5 minutes, then transfer to a wire rack and leave to cool completely.

**5** For the topping, put the green tea leaves into a jug, add about 75ml (2¹/₂fl oz) boiling water and leave to infuse for 5 minutes. Put the butter into a bowl and whisk until fluffy. Gradually add the icing sugar and whisk until combined. Pass the green tea through a sieve into the bowl, then discard the tea. Continue to whisk until light and fluffy.

**6** Insert a star nozzle into a piping bag, then fill the bag with the buttercream and pipe a swirl on to the top of each cake. Decorate each with a sugar flower.

## Freezing Tip

**To freeze** Complete the recipe to the end of step 4. Open-freeze, then wrap and freeze.

**To use** Thaw for about 1 hour, then complete the recipe.

| Serves | EASY | | NUTRITIONAL INFORMATION |
|---|---|---|---|
| **12** | **Preparation Time** 40 minutes | **Cooking Time** 25 minutes, plus cooling and infusing | **Per Cupcake** 282 calories; 13g fat (of which 8g saturates); 41g carbohydrate; 0.3g salt |

**Freezing Tip**

**To freeze** Complete the recipe to the end of step 3.
Open-freeze, then wrap and freeze.
**To use** Thaw for about 1 hour, then complete the recipe.

# Sweet Shop Cupcakes

175g (6oz) unsalted butter, softened
175g (6oz) caster sugar
3 medium eggs
175g (6oz) self-raising flour, sifted
grated zest of 1 lemon
½ tsp baking powder
125g (4oz) lemon curd

**ICING AND DECORATION**

75g (3oz) unsalted butter, softened
350g (12oz) icing sugar, sifted
50ml (2fl oz) milk
dolly mixtures, jelly beans or chocolate buttons

**1** Preheat the oven to 190°C (170°C fan oven), mark 5. Line a 12-hole muffin tin with paper muffin cases.

**2** Using a hand-held electric whisk, whisk the butter and caster sugar in a bowl, or beat with a wooden spoon, until pale and creamy. Gradually whisk in the eggs until just combined. Using a metal spoon, fold in the flour, lemon zest and baking powder until combined. Divide the mixture equally between the paper cases.

**3** Bake for 20 minutes or until golden and risen. Leave to cool in the tin for 5 minutes, then transfer to a wire rack to cool completely.

**4** Cut a small cone shape from the top of each cake. Put 1 tsp of lemon curd into the hole in each cake and then replace the cake cone, pressing down lightly.

**5** For the topping, put the butter into a bowl and whisk until fluffy. Gradually add half the icing sugar, whisking until combined. Add the milk and remaining icing sugar and whisk until light and fluffy, then, using a small palette knife, spread a little over each cake. Stand the cakes upright on the wire rack and leave for about 30 minutes to set. Decorate each cake with sweets when set.

| Serves | EASY | | NUTRITIONAL INFORMATION |
|---|---|---|---|
| **12** | **Preparation Time** 30 minutes | **Cooking Time** 20 minutes, plus cooling and setting | **Per Cupcake** 424 calories; 19g fat (of which 12g saturates); 64g carbohydrate; 0.6g salt |

## Freezing Tip

**To freeze** Complete the recipe to the end of step 4.
Open-freeze, then wrap and freeze.
**To use** Thaw for about 1 hour, then complete the recipe.

# Easter Cupcakes

2 medium eggs
75g (3oz) caster sugar
150ml (¼ pint) sunflower oil
150g (5oz) plain flour, sifted
½ tsp baking powder
1 tsp vanilla extract
15g (½oz) Rice Krispies

**TOPPING AND DECORATION**

100g (3½oz) white chocolate, broken into pieces
15g (½oz) unsalted butter
25g (1oz) Rice Krispies
12 chocolate mini eggs

**1** Preheat the oven to 180°C (160°C fan oven), mark 4. Line a 6-hole muffin tin with paper muffin cases.

**2** Separate the eggs, putting the whites in a clean, grease-free bowl and the yolks in another. Add the sugar to the yolks and whisk with a hand-held electric whisk until pale and creamy. Then whisk in the oil until combined.

**3** Whisk the egg whites until soft peaks form. Using a metal spoon, quickly fold the flour, baking powder, vanilla extract and Rice Krispies into the egg yolk mixture until just combined. Add half the egg whites to the egg yolk mixture to loosen, then carefully fold in the remaining egg whites. Divide the mixture equally between the paper cases.

**4** Bake for 20–25 minutes until golden and risen. Leave to cool in the tin for 5 minutes, then transfer to a wire rack to cool completely.

**5** For the topping, put the chocolate and butter into a heatproof bowl and place over a pan of barely simmering water, making sure the base of the bowl doesn't touch the water. Gently heat until the chocolate has melted, stirring occasionally until smooth. Remove the bowl from the heat, add the Rice Krispies and fold through until coated. Spoon the mixture on top of each cake, pressing down lightly, then top each with 2 chocolate eggs. Stand the cakes upright on the wire rack and leave for about 1 hour to set.

| EASY | | NUTRITIONAL INFORMATION | Serves |
|---|---|---|---|
| **Preparation Time**<br>30 minutes | **Cooking Time**<br>30 minutes, plus<br>cooling and setting | **Per Cupcake**<br>378 calories; 27g fat (of which 8g saturates);<br>32g carbohydrate; 0.2g salt | **6** |

# Truffle Kisses Cupcakes

150g (5oz) unsalted butter, softened
200g (7oz) caster sugar
3 medium eggs
75g (3oz) self-raising flour, sifted
200g (7oz) plain flour, sifted
1/2 tsp bicarbonate of soda
75g (3oz) roasted chopped hazelnuts
200ml (7fl oz) buttermilk
15g (1/2oz) plain chocolate, finely grated

**TOPPING AND DECORATION**
200ml (7fl oz) double cream
150g (5oz) plain chocolate
100g (3 1/2oz) milk chocolate, finely chopped
18 small chocolate truffles (optional)

1 Preheat the oven to 180°C (160°C fan oven), mark 4. Line a 12-hole and a 6-hole muffin tin with paper muffin cases.

2 Using a hand-held electric whisk, whisk the butter and sugar in a bowl, or beat with a wooden spoon, until pale and creamy. Gradually whisk in the eggs until just combined. Using a metal spoon, fold in both flours, the bicarbonate of soda, hazelnuts, buttermilk and grated chocolate until combined. Divide the mixture equally between the paper cases.

3 Bake for 20–25 minutes until golden and risen. Leave to cool in the tin for 5 minutes, then transfer to a wire rack to cool completely.

4 For the topping, heat the cream in a small saucepan until nearly boiling. Finely chop 100g (3 1/2oz) plain chocolate and put into a bowl along with all the milk chocolate. Pour the hot cream over the chocolate and leave to stand for 5 minutes, then stir gently until smooth. Chill the mixture for 15–20 minutes until thickened slightly.

5 Using a palette knife, spread a little chocolate cream over the top of each cake. Finely grate the remaining plain chocolate over the top of each cake. Finish each with a chocolate truffle, if you like. Stand the cakes upright on the wire rack and leave for about 1 hour to set.

## Freezing Tip

- - - - - - - - - - - - - - - - - - - - - - - - - - - - - - - - - - -

**To freeze** Complete the recipe to the end of step 3.
Open-freeze, then wrap and freeze.
**To use** Thaw for about 1 hour, then complete the recipe.

| EASY | | NUTRITIONAL INFORMATION | Serves |
|---|---|---|---|
| **Preparation Time** 40 minutes | **Cooking Time** 30 minutes, plus cooling and setting | **Per Cupcake** 317 calories; 20g fat (of which 10g saturates); 34g carbohydrate; 0.2g salt | **18** |

### Freezing Tip

--------------------------------------------------

**To freeze** Complete the recipe to the end of step 3.
Open-freeze, then wrap and freeze.
**To use** Thaw for about 1 hour, then complete the recipe.

# Honeycomb Cream Cupcakes

125g (4oz) unsalted butter, softened
50g (2oz) caster sugar
2 medium eggs
75g (3oz) runny honey
125g (4oz) self-raising flour, sifted
50g (2oz) rolled oats
$\frac{1}{2}$ tsp baking powder
1 tbsp milk

**ICING AND DECORATION**
125g (4oz) unsalted butter, softened
300g (11oz) golden icing sugar, sifted
2 tbsp milk
1 Crunchie bar, broken into shards

**1** Preheat the oven to 190°C (170°C fan oven), mark 5.
Line a 12-hole muffin tin with 9 paper muffin cases.

**2** Using a hand-held electric whisk, whisk the butter
and caster sugar in a bowl, or beat with a wooden
spoon, until pale and creamy. Gradually whisk in the
eggs and honey until just combined. Using a metal
spoon, fold in the flour, oats, baking powder and milk
until combined. Divide the mixture equally between
the paper cases.

**3** Bake for 20 minutes or until golden and risen. Cool in
the tin for 5 minutes, then transfer to a wire rack
and leave to cool completely.

**4** For the topping, put the butter into a bowl and whisk
until fluffy. Gradually whisk in half the icing sugar,
then add the milk and the remaining icing sugar and
whisk until light and fluffy.

**5** Insert a star nozzle into a piping bag, then fill the
bag with the buttercream and pipe a swirl on to the
top of each cake. When ready to serve, decorate each
with a few shards of Crunchie.

| Serves | EASY | | NUTRITIONAL INFORMATION |
|---|---|---|---|
| **9** | **Preparation Time** 30 minutes | **Cooking Time** 20 minutes, plus cooling | **Per Cupcake** 480 calories; 25g fat (of which 15g saturates); 65g carbohydrate; 0.6g salt |

## Freezing Tip

**To freeze** Complete the recipe to the end of step 3.
Open-freeze, then wrap and freeze.
**To use** Thaw for about 1 hour, then complete the recipe.

150g (5oz) unsalted butter, softened

175g (6oz) self-raising flour, sifted

50g (2oz) caster sugar

100g (3½oz) golden syrup

3 medium eggs

1 tsp baking powder

1 tsp ground mixed spice

50g (2oz) mixed chopped nuts

**TOPPING**

3 tbsp double cream

1 tbsp milk

50g (2oz) milk chocolate, finely chopped

25g (1oz) plain chocolate, finely chopped

75g (3oz) roasted chopped hazelnuts

# Nutty Cupcakes

**1** Preheat the oven to 190°C (170°C fan oven), mark 5. Line a 12-hole muffin tin with paper muffin cases.

**2** Using a hand-held electric whisk, whisk the butter, flour, sugar, syrup, eggs, baking powder, mixed spice and nuts in a large bowl until pale and creamy. Divide the mixture equally between the paper cases.

**3** Bake for 20 minutes or until golden and risen. Leave to cool in the tin for 5 minutes, then transfer to a wire rack to cool completely.

**4** For the topping, heat the cream and milk in a small saucepan until nearly boiling. Put both chocolates into a bowl and pour the hot cream over them. Leave to stand for 5 minutes, then gently stir until smooth.

**5** Put the hazelnuts into a shallow bowl. Dip the top of each cake into the chocolate cream, allow the excess to drip off, then dip into the hazelnuts until coated all over. Stand the cakes upright on the wire rack and leave for about 1 hour to set.

| EASY | | NUTRITIONAL INFORMATION | Serves |
|---|---|---|---|
| **Preparation Time** 40 minutes | **Cooking Time** 25 minutes, plus cooling and setting | **Per Cupcake** 338 calories; 23g fat (of which 10g saturates); 31g carbohydrate; 0.4g salt | **12** |

**Freezing Tip**

- - - - - - - - - - - - - - - - - - - - - - - - - - - - - - - - - - - - - - - - - -

**To freeze** Complete the recipe to the end of step 3.
Open-freeze, then wrap and freeze.
**To use** Thaw for about 1 hour, then complete the recipe.

# Jewelled Cupcakes

75g (3oz) unsalted butter, softened
150g (5oz) caster sugar
3 medium eggs
175g (6oz) self-raising flour, sifted
175g (6oz) mincemeat

**DECORATION**
75g (3oz) apricot jam
50g (2oz) toasted flaked almonds
50g (2oz) ready-to-eat apricots, chopped
12 glacé cherries
40g (1½oz) caster sugar
1 tbsp unsalted butter

**1** Preheat the oven to 190°C (170°C fan oven), mark 5. Line a 12-hole muffin tin with paper muffin cases.

**2** Using a hand-held electric whisk, whisk the butter and sugar in a bowl, or beat with a wooden spoon, until pale and creamy. Gradually whisk in the eggs until just combined. Using a metal spoon, fold in the flour and mincemeat until combined. Divide the mixture equally between the paper cases.

**3** Bake for 20 minutes or until golden and risen. Leave to cool in the tin for 5 minutes, then transfer to a wire rack to cool completely.

**4** For the decoration, brush each cake with a little apricot glaze, then scatter on a few almonds and apricots and a cherry. Stand the cakes upright on the wire rack.

**5** Put the sugar and 1 tbsp cold water into a small pan and gently heat until the sugar dissolves. Increase the heat and bubble for 3–4 minutes until the sugar caramelises and turns golden in colour. Remove from the heat and quickly stir in the butter until combined. Being very careful, drizzle the hot caramel over the top of each cake. Leave for about 10 minutes to set.

| Serves | EASY | | NUTRITIONAL INFORMATION |
|---|---|---|---|
| **12** | **Preparation Time** 40 minutes | **Cooking Time** 30 minutes, plus cooling and setting | **Per Serving** 276 calories; 10g fat (of which 4g saturates); 46g carbohydrate; 0.4g salt |

# Secret Garden Cupcakes

200g (7oz) fresh strawberries, hulled and halved
200g (7oz) caster sugar
150g (5oz) unsalted butter, softened
3 medium eggs
200g (7oz) self-raising flour, sifted
½ tsp bicarbonate of soda
50ml (2fl oz) buttermilk

### ICING

125g (4oz) unsalted butter, softened
250g (9oz) icing sugar, sifted
green food colouring
ladybird, bumble bee and butterfly sugar
decorations (optional)

**1** Preheat the oven to 190°C (170°C fan oven), mark 5. Line a 12-hole muffin tin with paper muffin cases.

**2** Put the strawberries and 50g (2oz) caster sugar into a heatproof bowl and cover with clingfilm. Put over a pan of barely simmering water and cook gently for 30 minutes.

**3** Meanwhile, using a hand-held electric whisk, whisk the butter and remaining caster sugar in a bowl, or beat with a wooden spoon, until pale and creamy. Gradually whisk in the eggs until just combined. Using a metal spoon, fold in the flour, bicarbonate of soda and buttermilk until combined. Divide the mixture equally between the paper cases.

**4** Bake for 20 minutes or until golden and risen. Leave to cool in the tin for 5 minutes. Meanwhile, pass the strawberries and juice through a sieve into a shallow bowl. Discard the strawberries.

**5** Using a cocktail stick, prick the top of the cakes all over. Dip the top of each cake into the strawberry syrup, then transfer to a wire rack to cool completely.

**6** For the topping, put the butter into a bowl and whisk until fluffy. Gradually whisk in half the icing sugar, then add 1 tbsp boiling water, a little green food colouring and the remaining icing sugar and whisk until light and fluffy.

**7** Insert a star nozzle into a piping bag, then fill the bag with the buttercream and pipe in a zigzag pattern on top of each cake. Decorate with the sugar ladybirds, butterflies and bumble bees, if you like.

| EASY | | NUTRITIONAL INFORMATION | Serves |
|---|---|---|---|
| **Preparation Time** 35 minutes | **Cooking Time** 50 minutes, plus cooling | **Per Cupcake** 398 calories; 20g fat (of which 13g saturates); 53g carbohydrate; 0.5g salt | **12** |

**Freezing Tip**

------------------------------------------------------

**To freeze** Complete the recipe to the end of step 3.
Open-freeze, then wrap and freeze.
**To use** Thaw for about 1 hour, then complete the recipe.

# Aniseed Cupcakes

125g (4oz) unsalted butter, softened
200g (7oz) caster sugar
2 medium eggs
200g (7oz) self-raising flour, sifted
25g (1oz) custard powder
2 tbsp caraway seeds
125ml (4fl oz) milk

### ICING AND DECORATION

75g (3oz) unsalted butter, softened
300g (11oz) icing sugar, sifted
2 tbsp Pernod
pale blue sugar balls

**1** Preheat the oven to 190°C (170°C fan oven), mark 5. Line a 12-hole muffin tin with paper muffin cases.

**2** Using a hand-held electric whisk, whisk the butter and caster sugar in a bowl, or beat with a wooden spoon, until pale and creamy. Gradually whisk in the eggs until just combined. Using a metal spoon, fold in the flour, custard powder, caraway seeds and milk until combined. Divide the mixture equally between the paper cases.

**3** Bake for 20–25 minutes until golden and risen. Leave to cool in the tin for 5 minutes, then transfer to a wire rack to cool completely.

**4** For the topping, put the butter into a bowl and whisk until fluffy. Gradually whisk in half the icing sugar, then add the Pernod, 1 tbsp boiling water and the remaining icing sugar and whisk until light and fluffy. Using a small palette knife, spread a little of the buttercream over the top of each cake, then sprinkle with the blue sugar balls.

| Serves | EASY | | NUTRITIONAL INFORMATION |
|---|---|---|---|
| **12** | **Preparation Time** 30 minutes | **Cooking Time** 20–25 minutes, plus cooling | **Per Cupcake** 291 calories; 15g fat (of which 9g saturates); 37g carbohydrate; 0.4g salt |

## Freezing Tip

------------------------------------------------

**To freeze** Complete the recipe to the end of step 3.
Open-freeze, then wrap and freeze.
**To use** Thaw for about 1 hour, then complete the recipe.

175g (6oz) self-raising flour, sifted

$\frac{1}{2}$ tsp bicarbonate of soda

150g (5oz) light soft brown sugar

1 banana (about 150g/5oz), peeled

3 medium eggs

100g (3$\frac{1}{2}$oz) unsalted butter, melted

75ml (2$\frac{1}{2}$fl oz) buttermilk

**ICING AND DECORATION**

150g (5oz) dulce de leche toffee sauce

75g (3oz) unsalted butter, softened

250g (9oz) golden icing sugar, sifted

mini fudge chunks (optional)

# Banoffee Cupcakes

**1** Preheat the oven to 190°C (170°C fan oven), mark 5. Line a 12-hole muffin tin with paper muffin cases.

**2** Put the flour, bicarbonate of soda and brown sugar into a large bowl. Mash the banana with a fork in a small bowl. Put the eggs, melted butter and buttermilk into a jug and lightly beat together until combined. Pour into the flour mixture along with the mashed banana and stir with a spatula until just combined. Divide the mixture equally between the paper cases.

**3** Bake for 18–20 minutes until lightly golden and risen. Cool in the tin for 5 minutes, then transfer to a wire rack and leave to cool completely.

**4** For the decoration, whisk together the dulce de leche and butter in a bowl until combined. Gradually whisk in the icing sugar until light and fluffy. Use a palette knife to spread the buttercream on to the top of each cake. Decorate with the mini fudge chunks, if you like.

| EASY | | NUTRITIONAL INFORMATION | Serves |
|---|---|---|---|
| **Preparation Time** 30 minutes | **Cooking Time** 18–20 minutes, plus cooling | **Per Cupcake** 404 calories; 16g fat (of which 10g saturates); 63g carbohydrate; 0.4g salt | **12** |

# Pretty Pink Cupcakes

150g (5oz) raw beetroot, peeled and finely grated

200g (7oz) self-raising flour, sifted

1/2 tsp bicarbonate of soda

150g (5oz) caster sugar

grated zest of 1 orange

2 medium eggs

100ml (3½fl oz) sunflower oil

125ml (4fl oz) buttermilk

**ICING AND DECORATION**

100g (3½oz) unsalted butter, softened

350g (12oz) icing sugar, sifted

50ml (2fl oz) milk

pink food colouring

ready-made pink or red sugar flowers (optional)

**1** Preheat the oven to 190°C (170°C fan oven), mark 5. Line a 12-hole muffin tin with paper muffin cases.

**2** Put the beetroot, flour, bicarbonate of soda, caster sugar and orange zest into a bowl. Put the eggs, oil and buttermilk into a jug and lightly beat together until combined. Pour the egg mixture into the flour and stir with a spatula until just combined. Divide the mixture equally between the paper cases.

**3** Bake for 20 minutes or until lightly golden and risen. Cool in the tin for 5 minutes, then transfer to a wire rack and leave to cool completely.

**4** For the topping, put the butter into a bowl and whisk until fluffy. Gradually whisk in half the icing sugar, then add the milk, a little pink food colouring and the remaining icing sugar and whisk until light and fluffy.

**5** Insert a star nozzle into a piping bag, then fill the bag with the buttercream and pipe small swirls all the way around the top of each cake. Decorate with the sugar flowers, if you like.

## Freezing Tip

**To freeze** Complete the recipe to the end of step 3. Open-freeze, then wrap and freeze.
**To use** Thaw for about 1 hour, then complete the recipe.

| EASY | | NUTRITIONAL INFORMATION | Serves |
|---|---|---|---|
| **Preparation Time** 35 minutes | **Cooking Time** 20 minutes, plus cooling | **Per Cupcake** 361 calories; 14g fat (of which 6g saturates); 58g carbohydrate; 0.2g salt | **12** |

### Freezing Tip

**To freeze** Complete the recipe to the end of step 3. Open-freeze, then wrap and freeze.
**To use** Thaw for about 1 hour, then complete the recipe.

# Marbled Chocolate Cupcakes

75g (3oz) unsalted butter, softened
150g (5oz) caster sugar
2 medium eggs
25g (1oz) self-raising flour, sifted
125g (4oz) plain flour, sifted
½ tsp bicarbonate of soda
2 tsp vanilla extract
150ml (¼ pint) buttermilk
25g (1oz) cocoa powder, sifted

**ICING**

125g (4oz) unsalted butter, softened
350g (12oz) icing sugar, sifted
2 tsp vanilla extract
2 tbsp cocoa powder, sifted

**1** Preheat the oven to 190°C (170°C fan oven), mark 5. Line a 12-hole muffin tin with paper muffin cases.

**2** Using a hand-held electric whisk, whisk the butter and caster sugar in a bowl, or beat with a wooden spoon, until pale and creamy. Gradually whisk in the eggs until just combined. Using a metal spoon, fold in both flours, the bicarbonate of soda, vanilla extract and buttermilk until combined. Put half this mixture into another bowl and whisk in the cocoa powder. Then very lightly fold this mixture into the vanilla mixture, to create a marbled effect. Divide the mixture equally between the paper cases.

**3** Bake for 20 minutes or until golden and risen. Leave to cool in the tin for 5 minutes, then transfer to a wire rack to cool completely.

**4** For the topping, put the butter into a bowl and whisk until fluffy. Gradually whisk in half the icing sugar, then add the vanilla extract, 2 tbsp boiling water and the remaining icing sugar and whisk until light and fluffy. Put half the mixture into another bowl and whisk in the cocoa powder.

**5** Insert a star nozzle into a piping bag, then fill the bag alternately with the vanilla and chocolate buttercreams. Pipe a swirl on to the top of each cake.

| Serves | EASY | | NUTRITIONAL INFORMATION |
|---|---|---|---|
| **12** | **Preparation Time** 40 minutes | **Cooking Time** 20 minutes, plus cooling | **Per Cupcake** 360 calories; 16g fat (of which 10g saturates); 54g carbohydrate; 0.5g salt |

### Freezing Tip

**To freeze** Complete the recipe to the end of step 4.
Open-freeze, then wrap and freeze.
**To use** Thaw for about 1 hour, then complete the recipe.

# Sea Breeze Cupcakes

1 pink grapefruit (about 350g/12oz)
50g (2oz) ready-to-eat dried cranberries
250g (9oz) self-raising flour, sifted
125g (4oz) caster sugar
50ml (2fl oz) milk
1 medium egg, beaten
75g (3oz) unsalted butter, melted
1 tsp baking powder

**ICING AND DECORATION**
300g (11oz) fondant icing sugar, sifted
red and yellow food colouring
50g (2oz) apricot jam
edible silver balls
cocktail umbrellas (optional)

**1** Preheat the oven to 190°C (170°C fan oven), mark 5. Line a 12-hole muffin tin with paper muffin cases.

**2** Grate the zest from half the grapefruit into a bowl. Set aside. Cut the top and bottom off the grapefruit and stand it upright on a board. Using a serrated knife, cut away the pith in a downward motion. Cut in between the membranes to remove the segments. Whiz the segments in a food processor until puréed.

**3** Transfer the purée into the bowl with the zest. Add the cranberries, flour, caster sugar, milk, egg, melted butter and baking powder and stir with a spatula until just combined. Divide the mixture equally between the paper cases.

**4** Bake for 20 minutes or until golden and risen. Leave to cool in the tin for 5 minutes, then transfer to a wire rack to cool completely.

**5** For the icing, put the icing sugar into a bowl and add enough water (2–4 tbsp) to make a smooth icing. Add a few drops of food colouring to make it pinky-orange in colour. Brush the tops of the cakes with the apricot glaze, then spoon a little icing on to each cake to flood the top. Decorate with the silver balls. Stand the cakes upright on the wire rack and leave for about 1 hour to set. Decorate with a cocktail umbrella once set, if you like.

| EASY | | NUTRITIONAL INFORMATION | Serves |
|---|---|---|---|
| **Preparation Time**<br>40 minutes | **Cooking Time**<br>20 minutes, plus<br>cooling and setting | **Per Cupcake**<br>287 calories;6g fat (of which 4g saturates);<br>61g carbohydrate; 0.1g salt | **12** |

# 2

# Muffins and Small Cakes

Bran and Apple Muffins

Blueberry Muffins

Wholemeal Banana Muffins

Brown Sugar Muffins

Cherry and Almond Muffins

Spiced Carrot Muffins

White Chocolate Scones with Summer Berries

Chocolate Banana Muffins

Honey and Yogurt Muffins

Brazil Nut and Clementine Cakes

Chocolate Butterfly Cakes

Apple Madeleines

### Freezing Tip

**To freeze** Complete the recipe, but don't sprinkle with the sugar topping. Once the muffins are cold, pack, seal and freeze.

**To use** Thaw at cool room temperature. Sprinkle with the sugar to serve.

# Bran and Apple Muffins

250ml (9fl oz) semi-skimmed milk

2 tbsp orange juice

50g (2oz) All Bran

9 ready-to-eat dried prunes

100g (3½oz) light muscovado sugar

2 medium egg whites

1 tbsp golden syrup

150g (5oz) plain flour, sifted

1 tsp baking powder

1 tsp ground cinnamon

1 eating apple, peeled and grated

demerara sugar to sprinkle

**1** Preheat the oven to 190°C (170°C fan oven) mark 5. Line a 12-hole bun tin or muffin tin with 10 paper muffin cases.

**2** Put the milk, orange juice and All Bran into a bowl and stir to mix. Put to one side for 10 minutes.

**3** Put the prunes into a food processor or blender with 100ml (3½fl oz) water and whiz for 2–3 minutes to make a purée, then add the muscovado sugar and whiz briefly to mix.

**4** Put the egg whites into a clean, grease-free bowl and whisk until soft peaks form. Add the whites to the milk mixture with the syrup, flour, baking powder, cinnamon, grated apple and prune mixture. Fold all the ingredients together gently – don't overmix. Spoon the mixture into the muffin cases.

**5** Bake for 30 minutes or until well risen and golden brown. Transfer to a wire rack and leave to cool completely. Sprinkle with demerara sugar just before serving. These are best eaten on the day they are made.

| Serves | EASY | | NUTRITIONAL INFORMATION |
|---|---|---|---|
| **10** | **Preparation Time** 10 minutes | **Cooking Time** 30 minutes, plus cooling | **Per Muffin** 137 calories; 1g fat (of which trace saturates); 31g carbohydrate; 0.3g salt |

## Freezing Tip

**To freeze** Complete the recipe. Once the muffins are cold, pack, seal and freeze.
**To use** Thaw at cool room temperature.

## Try Something Different

**Double Chocolate Chip Muffins:** Omit the blueberries and lemon zest. Replace 40g (1½oz) of the flour with cocoa powder, then add 150g (5oz) chopped dark chocolate to the dry ingredients in step 3.

# Blueberry Muffins

2 medium eggs
250ml (9fl oz) semi-skimmed milk
250g (9oz) golden granulated sugar
2 tsp vanilla extract
350g (12oz) plain flour
4 tsp baking powder
250g (9oz) blueberries, frozen
finely grated zest of 2 lemons

**1** Preheat the oven to 200°C (180°C fan oven) mark 6. Line a 12-hole bun tin or muffin tin with 10 paper muffin cases.

**2** Put the eggs, milk, sugar and vanilla extract into a bowl and mix well.

**3** In another bowl, sift the flour and baking powder together, then add the blueberries and lemon zest. Toss together and make a well in the centre.

**4** Pour the egg mixture into the flour and blueberries and mix in gently – overbeating will make the muffins tough. Divide the mixture equally between the paper cases.

**5** Bake for 20–25 minutes until risen and just firm. Transfer to a wire rack and leave to cool completely. These are best eaten on the day they are made.

| EASY | | NUTRITIONAL INFORMATION | Serves |
|---|---|---|---|
| **Preparation Time** 10 minutes | **Cooking Time** 20–25 minutes, plus cooling | **Per Muffin** 218 calories; 2g fat (of which trace saturates); 49g carbohydrate; 0.5g salt | **10** |

# Wholemeal Banana Muffins

50g (2oz) raisins

finely grated zest and juice of 1 orange

125g (4oz) wholemeal flour

25g (1oz) wheatgerm

3 tbsp caster sugar

2 tsp baking powder

pinch of salt

1 large egg, beaten

50ml (2fl oz) milk

50ml (2fl oz) sunflower oil

2 medium-sized ripe bananas, about 225g (8oz) when peeled, roughly mashed

**TOPPING**

5 tbsp orange marmalade

50g (2oz) banana chips, roughly chopped

50g (2oz) walnuts, roughly chopped

**1** Preheat the oven to 200°C (180°C fan oven) mark 6. Line a 6-hole bun tin or muffin tin with paper muffin cases. Put the raisins into a bowl, pour the orange juice over them and leave to soak for 1 hour.

**2** Put the orange zest into a bowl with the flour, wheatgerm, sugar, baking powder and salt and mix together. Make a well in the centre.

**3** In a separate bowl, mix the egg, milk and oil, then pour into the flour mixture and stir until just blended. Drain the raisins, reserving 1 tbsp juice, and stir into the mixture with the bananas. Don't overmix. Fill each muffin case two-thirds full.

**4** Bake for 20–25 minutes until a skewer inserted into the centre comes out clean. Transfer to a wire rack and leave to cool slightly.

**5** For the topping, gently heat the marmalade with the reserved orange juice until melted. Simmer for 1 minute, then add the banana chips and walnuts. Spoon on top of the muffins. Serve while still warm.

## Freezing Tip

**To freeze** Complete the recipe to the end of step 4. Once the muffins are cold, pack, seal and freeze.
**To use** Thaw at cool room temperature. Complete the recipe.

| EASY | | NUTRITIONAL INFORMATION | Serves |
|---|---|---|---|
| **Preparation Time** 15 minutes, plus soaking | **Cooking Time** 25–30 minutes | **Per Muffin** 341 calories; 13g fat (of which 2g saturates); 51g carbohydrate; 0.6g salt | **6** |

## Try Something Different

**Apple and Cinnamon Muffins:** Fold 5 tbsp ready-made chunky apple sauce and 1 tsp ground cinnamon into the mixture with the flour.

**Maple Syrup and Pecan Muffins:** Lightly toast 50g (2oz) pecan nuts and roughly chop. Fold half the nuts and 3 tbsp maple syrup into the mixture. Mix the remaining nuts with the crushed sugar and sprinkle over the muffins before baking. Drizzle with maple syrup to serve.

## Freezing Tip

**To freeze** Complete the recipe. Once the muffins are cold, pack, seal and freeze.
**To use** Thaw at cool room temperature.

12 brown sugar cubes
150g (5oz) plain flour
1$\frac{1}{2}$ tsp baking powder
$\frac{1}{4}$ tsp salt
1 medium egg, beaten
40g (1$\frac{1}{2}$oz) golden caster sugar
50g (2oz) unsalted butter, melted
$\frac{1}{2}$ tsp vanilla extract
100ml (3$\frac{1}{2}$fl oz) milk

# Brown Sugar Muffins

**1** Preheat the oven to 200°C (180°C fan oven) mark 6. Line a 6-hole bun tin or muffin tin with paper muffin cases.

**2** Roughly crush the sugar cubes and put to one side. Sift the flour, baking powder and salt together.

**3** Put the beaten egg, caster sugar, melted butter, vanilla extract and milk into a large bowl and stir to combine. Gently fold in the sifted flour. Spoon the mixture equally into the paper cases and sprinkle with the brown sugar.

**4** Bake for 30–35 minutes until golden. Transfer to a wire rack and leave to cool completely. These are best eaten on the day they are made.

| Serves 6 | EASY | | NUTRITIONAL INFORMATION |
|---|---|---|---|
| | **Preparation Time** 10 minutes | **Cooking Time** 30–35 minutes, plus cooling | **Per Muffin** 233 calories; 8g fat (of which 5g saturates); 38g carbohydrate; 0.4g salt |

**Freezing Tip**

**To freeze** Complete the recipe. Once the muffins are cold, pack, seal and freeze.
**To use** Thaw at cool room temperature.

# Cherry and Almond Muffins

225g (8oz) plain flour
1 tsp baking powder
pinch of salt
75g (3oz) caster sugar
50g (2oz) ground almonds
350g (12oz) glacé cherries, roughly chopped
300ml (½ pint) milk
3 tbsp lemon juice
50ml (2fl oz) sunflower oil or melted butter
1 large egg
1 tsp almond extract
roughly crushed sugar cubes to decorate

**1** Preheat the oven to 190°C (170°C fan oven) mark 5. Line a 12-hole bun tin or muffin tin with paper muffin cases.

**2** Sift the flour, baking powder and salt together. Add the caster sugar and ground almonds, then stir in the chopped cherries.

**3** Whisk the milk, lemon juice, oil or butter, the egg and almond extract together. Pour into the dry ingredients and stir until all the ingredients are just combined – the mixture should be lumpy. Do not overmix or the muffins will be tough. Spoon the mixture equally into the paper cases and sprinkle with the crushed sugar cubes.

**4** Bake for about 25 minutes or until golden and well risen.

**5** Leave to cool in the tin for 5 minutes, then transfer to a wire rack to cool completely. These are best eaten on the day they are made.

| EASY | | NUTRITIONAL INFORMATION | Serves |
|---|---|---|---|
| **Preparation Time** 10 minutes | **Cooking Time** 25 minutes, plus cooling | **Per Muffin** 230 calories; 6g fat (of which 1g saturates); 42g carbohydrate; 0.1g salt | **12** |

**Freezing Tip**

**To freeze** Complete the recipe to the end of step 3. Once the muffins are cold, pack, seal and freeze.
**To use** Thaw at cool room temperature and complete the recipe.

# Spiced Carrot Muffins

125g (4oz) unsalted butter, softened
125g (4oz) light muscovado sugar
3 pieces preserved stem ginger, drained and chopped
150g (5oz) self-raising flour, sifted
1½ tsp baking powder
1 tbsp ground mixed spice
25g (1oz) ground almonds
3 medium eggs
finely grated zest of ½ orange
150g (5oz) carrots, peeled and grated
50g (2oz) pecan nuts, chopped
50g (2oz) sultanas
3 tbsp white rum or orange liqueur (optional)

**TOPPING AND DECORATION**
200g (7oz) cream cheese
75g (3oz) icing sugar
1 tsp lemon juice
12 unsprayed rose petals (optional)

**1** Preheat the oven to 180°C (160°C fan oven) mark 4. Line a 12-hole bun tin or muffin tin with paper muffin cases.

**2** Beat the butter, muscovado sugar and stem ginger together until pale and creamy. Add the flour, baking powder, spice, ground almonds, eggs and orange zest and beat well until combined. Stir in the carrots, pecan nuts and sultanas. Divide the mixture equally among the paper cases.

**3** Bake for 20–25 minutes until risen and just firm. A skewer inserted into the centre should come out clean. Transfer to a wire rack and leave to cool completely.

**4** For the topping, beat the cream cheese in a bowl until softened. Beat in the icing sugar and lemon juice to give a smooth icing that just holds its shape.

**5** Drizzle each cake with a little liqueur, if using. Using a small palette knife, spread a little icing over each cake. Decorate with a rose petal, if you like.

| Serves | EASY | | NUTRITIONAL INFORMATION |
| --- | --- | --- | --- |
| **12** | **Preparation Time** 30 minutes | **Cooking Time** 20–25 minutes, plus cooling | **Per Muffin** 333 calories; 22g fat (of which 11g saturates); 31g carbohydrate; 0.5g salt |

# White Chocolate Scones with Summer Berries

150g (5oz) mixed summer berries, such as strawberries, raspberries, blackberries and currants

1 tbsp lemon juice

3 tbsp redcurrant or blackcurrant jelly

75g (3oz) unsalted butter, diced, plus extra to grease

225g (8oz) self-raising flour, plus extra to dust

½ tsp baking powder

1 tbsp golden caster sugar

1 x 125g (4oz) good-quality white chocolate, finely chopped

1 medium egg, beaten

6 tbsp milk

142ml tub clotted cream, or lightly whipped cream

icing sugar to dust

**1** Put the berries into a small bowl, slicing the strawberries if you're using them. Heat the lemon juice and jelly in a small pan, stirring until syrupy and smooth. Pour over the berries and put to one side to cool.

**2** Preheat the oven to 200°C (180°C fan oven) mark 6. Lightly grease a baking sheet.

**3** Put the flour, baking powder and caster sugar into a large bowl. Rub in the butter, then stir in the chocolate. Make a well in the centre, then add the egg and milk. Stir lightly with a round-bladed knife until the mixture just comes together into a soft dough – add a splash more milk if it looks too dry.

**4** Turn out on to a floured surface and press into a rough round about 2.5cm (1in) deep – the dough doesn't need to be too smooth. Stamp out small rounds using a 4cm (1½in) cutter and put on the prepared baking sheet.

**5** Bake the scones for 10–15 minutes until risen and golden, then remove from the oven and transfer to a wire rack to cool.

**6** To serve, split open the scones and spread with clotted or whipped cream. Add a small spoonful of fruit, replace the tops and dust with icing sugar. These are best eaten on the day they are made.

| EASY | | NUTRITIONAL INFORMATION | Serves |
| --- | --- | --- | --- |
| **Preparation Time** 20 minutes | **Cooking Time** 15–20 minutes, plus cooling | **Per Scone** 195 calories; 13g fat (of which 8g saturates); 19g carbohydrate; 0.3g salt | **16** |

# Chocolate Banana Muffins

275g (10oz) self-raising flour
1 tsp bicarbonate of soda
½ tsp salt
3 large bananas, about 450g (1lb)
125g (4oz) golden caster sugar
1 large egg, beaten
50ml (2fl oz) semi-skimmed milk
75g (3oz) unsalted butter, melted and cooled
50g (2oz) plain chocolate, chopped

**1** Preheat the oven to 180°C (160°C fan oven) mark 4. Line a 12-hole bun tin or muffin tin with paper muffin cases.

**2** Sift the flour, bicarbonate of soda and salt together into a large mixing bowl and put to one side.

**3** Peel the bananas and mash with a fork in a bowl. Add the caster sugar, egg, milk and melted butter and mix until well combined. Add this to the flour mixture, with the chopped chocolate. Stir gently, using only a few strokes, until the flour is only just incorporated – do not overmix. The mixture should be lumpy. Spoon the mixture equally into the paper cases, half-filling them.

**4** Bake for 20 minutes or until the muffins are well risen and golden. Transfer to a wire rack to cool completely. Serve warm or cold. These are best eaten on the day they are made.

| Serves 12 | EASY | | NUTRITIONAL INFORMATION |
|---|---|---|---|
| | **Preparation Time** 15 minutes | **Cooking Time** 20 minutes, plus cooling | **Per Muffin** 228 calories; 7g fat (of which 4g saturates); 40g carbohydrate; 0.5g salt |

## Freezing Tip

**To freeze** Complete the recipe. Once the muffins are cold, pack, seal and freeze.
**To use** Thaw at cool room temperature.

225g (8oz) plain flour

1½ tsp baking powder

1 tsp bicarbonate of soda

½ tsp each ground mixed spice and ground nutmeg

pinch of salt

50g (2oz) ground oatmeal

50g (2oz) light muscovado sugar

225g (8oz) Greek-style yogurt

125ml (4fl oz) milk

1 medium egg

50g (2oz) butter, melted and cooled

4 tbsp runny honey

# Honey and Yogurt Muffins

**1** Preheat the oven to 200°C (180°C fan oven) mark 6. Line a 12-hole bun tin or muffin tin with paper muffin cases.

**2** Sift the flour, baking powder, bicarbonate of soda, mixed spice, nutmeg and salt into a bowl. Stir in the oatmeal and sugar.

**3** Mix the yogurt with the milk in a bowl, then beat in the egg, butter and honey. Pour on to the dry ingredients and stir in quickly until just blended – don't overmix. Divide the mixture equally between the paper cases.

**4** Bake for 17–20 minutes until the muffins are well risen and just firm. Cool in the tin for 5 minutes, then transfer to a wire rack. Serve warm or cold. These are best eaten on the day they are made.

| EASY | | NUTRITIONAL INFORMATION | Serves |
|---|---|---|---|
| **Preparation Time** 15 minutes | **Cooking Time** 17–20 minutes, plus cooling | **Per Muffin** 180 calories; 6g fat (of which 4g saturates); 27g carbohydrate; 0.1g salt | **12** |

# Brazil Nut and Clementine Cakes

butter to grease

1 lemon

10 clementines

150g (5oz) brazil nuts

100ml (3½fl oz) mild olive oil

3 medium eggs

275g (10oz) golden caster sugar

1 tsp baking powder

2 tbsp brandy

### DECORATION

mint sprigs

icing sugar

**1** Grease eight 150ml (¼ pint) ramekin dishes and base-line with greaseproof paper. Wash the lemon and 4 clementines and put into a pan. Cover with boiling water, reduce the heat to a gentle simmer and cook for 30 minutes or until the clementines are tender.

**2** Remove the clementines with a slotted spoon and set aside. Cook the lemon for a further 10 minutes or until tender. Drain, reserving 200ml (7fl oz) liquid, and cool slightly. Halve the fruit, remove the pips and roughly chop.

**3** Preheat the oven to 180°C (160°C fan oven) mark 4. Whiz the nuts in a food processor until finely chopped, then tip out and set aside. There's no need to wash the jug – add the cooked fruit and blend to a purée.

**4** Put the oil, eggs and 125g (4oz) caster sugar into a mixing bowl and whisk until slightly thick and foamy. Stir in the ground nuts, fruit purée and baking powder. Divide among the ramekins and put on a baking sheet. Bake for 25 minutes or until slightly risen and firm to the touch. Leave to cool in the ramekins.

**5** Peel the remaining clementines, remove the pips and divide into segments, then skin each segment. Heat the remaining sugar in a small pan with 150ml (¼ pint) of the reserved cooking liquid until the sugar dissolves. Bring to the boil and cook until a pale caramel in colour. Dip the base of the pan into cold water to stop the caramel cooking. Stir in the remaining liquid and the brandy. Return to the heat, stirring until the caramel has dissolved. Stir in the clementine segments.

**6** Loosen the edges of the cakes, turn out on to individual plates and remove the paper lining. Pile the fruit segments on top and spoon the caramel over them. Decorate each with a mint sprig and a dusting of icing sugar.

| Serves | EASY | | NUTRITIONAL INFORMATION |
|---|---|---|---|
| | **Preparation Time** | **Cooking Time** | **Per Cake** |
| 8 | 30 minutes | 1¼ hours, plus cooling | 413 calories; 26g fat (of which 5g saturates); 41g carbohydrate; 0.1g salt |

**Cook's Tip**

Colour the buttercream with pink or green food colouring if you like, to match the theme of the party.

# Chocolate Butterfly Cakes

125g (4oz) unsalted butter, very soft

125g (4oz) caster sugar

2 medium eggs, lightly beaten individually

125g (4oz) plain flour

25g (1oz) cocoa powder

½ tsp baking powder

1 tbsp milk

1 x quantity of buttercream icing (see page 27)

**1** Preheat the oven to 190°C (170°C fan oven) mark 5. Put 18 cake cases into 2 bun trays.

**2** Using a hand-held electric whisk, beat the butter and sugar together until soft and fluffy and lighter in colour. Beat in the eggs thoroughly, one at a time.

**3** Sift the flour, cocoa powder and baking powder into the bowl and fold in gently until well mixed. Fold in the milk to give a soft, dropping consistency. Divide the mixture equally between the paper cases.

**4** Bake for 15–20 minutes until risen and firm. Transfer to a wire rack to cool completely.

**5** Slice off the top of each cake and cut the slice in half. Using a palette knife, spread buttercream on each cake. Put the 'butterfly wings' on top, with their curved sides facing towards each other.

| Serves | EASY | | NUTRITIONAL INFORMATION |
|---|---|---|---|
| **18** | **Preparation Time** 25 minutes | **Cooking Time** 15–20 minutes, plus cooling | **Per Cake** 170 calories; 7g fat (of which 4g saturates); 26g carbohydrate; 0.2g salt |

# Apple Madeleines

150g (5oz) unsalted butter, melted and cooled, plus extra to grease

3 large eggs

150g (5oz) caster sugar

1 tsp vanilla extract

150g (5oz) plain flour, sifted

½ tsp baking powder

2 apples such as Cox's, peeled, cored and finely chopped

icing sugar to dust

**1** Preheat the oven to 200°C (180°C fan oven) mark 6. Grease the madeleine tins.

**2** Put the eggs and caster sugar into a bowl and, using a hand-held electric whisk, beat together until thick (this should take about 8 minutes), then add the vanilla extract. Quickly but gently, fold in the flour, baking powder and apples followed by the melted butter, making sure the butter doesn't settle at the bottom of the bowl. Spoon the mixture equally into the madeleine tins.

**3** Bake for 8–10 minutes until golden, then remove from the tins and transfer to wire racks to cool completely. Dust with icing sugar before serving.

| EASY | | NUTRITIONAL INFORMATION | Serves |
|---|---|---|---|
| **Preparation Time** 15 minutes | **Cooking Time** 8–10 minutes, plus cooling | **Per Madeleine** 106 calories; 6g fat (of which 4g saturates); 13g carbohydrate; 0.1g salt | **24** |

# 3

# Brownies and Traybakes

Double-chocolate Brownies
The Ultimate Chocolate Brownie
Blackberry Traybake
Carrot Traybake
White Chocolate and Nut Brownies
Chocolate Pecan Bars
Cherry Chocolate Fudge Brownies
Muesli Bars
Low-fat Brownies
Apricot and Almond Traybake
Quick Chocolate Slices
Figgy Fruit Slice
Lamingtons
Chocolate Fudge Brownies
Hazelnut and Chocolate Flapjacks
Sticky Ginger Flapjacks
Fruit and Nut Flapjack
Raspberry and Cream Cheese
Chocolate Brownies
Vanilla Crumble Bars

# Double-chocolate Brownies

250g (9oz) butter, plus extra to grease

250g (9oz) plain chocolate (at least 50% cocoa solids), broken into pieces

100g (3½oz) white chocolate, broken into pieces

4 medium eggs

175g (6oz) light muscovado sugar

1 tsp vanilla extract

75g (3oz) plain flour, sifted

¼ tsp baking powder

1 tbsp cocoa powder, sifted, plus extra to dust (optional)

100g (3½oz) pecan nuts, chopped

pinch of salt

icing sugar to dust (optional)

vanilla ice cream to serve

**1** Preheat the oven to 200°C (180°C fan oven) mark 6. Grease a 20.5cm (8 inch) square shallow tin and base-line with baking parchment. Melt the butter and plain chocolate in a heatproof bowl set over a pan of gently simmering water, making sure the base of the bowl doesn't touch the water. Remove the bowl from the pan and put to one side.

**2** In a separate bowl, melt the white chocolate over a pan of gently simmering water, making sure the base of the bowl doesn't touch the water. Remove the bowl from the pan and put to one side.

**3** Put the eggs into a separate large bowl. Add the muscovado sugar and vanilla extract and whisk together until the mixture is pale and thick.

**4** Add the flour, baking powder, cocoa powder, the pecan nuts and salt to the bowl, then carefully pour in the plain chocolate mixture. Using a large metal spoon, gently fold the ingredients together to make a smooth batter – if you fold too roughly, the chocolate will seize up and become unusable.

**5** Pour the brownie mixture into the prepared tin. Spoon dollops of the white chocolate over the brownie mix, then swirl a skewer through it several times to create a marbled effect.

**6** Bake for 20–25 minutes. The brownie should be fudgy inside and the top should be cracked and crispy. Leave to cool in the tin.

**7** Transfer to a board and cut into 16 individual brownies. To serve, dust with a little icing sugar and cocoa powder or serve with ice cream.

## Try Something Different

Try making these brownies without butter – believe it or not, this recipe will still work. But you'll need to eat them within an hour of taking them out of the oven – fat is what makes cakes moist and allows them to be stored.

## Note

For convenience, complete the recipe to the end of step 6, then store in an airtight container. It will keep for up to one week. Complete the recipe to serve.

| EASY | | NUTRITIONAL INFORMATION | Serves |
|---|---|---|---|
| **Preparation Time** 15 minutes | **Cooking Time** 20–25 minutes, plus cooling | **Per Brownie** 352 calories; 25g fat (of which 13g saturates); 29g carbohydrate; 0.3g salt | **16** |

**Cook's Tip**

The secret to really moist, squidgy brownies is all in the timing. A few minutes too long in the oven will produce a dry texture, so be careful not to bake them for too long.

# The Ultimate Chocolate Brownie

200g (7oz) salted butter, plus extra to grease
400g (14oz) good-quality plain chocolate
225g (8oz) light muscovado sugar
1 tsp vanilla extract
150g (5oz) pecan nuts, roughly chopped
25g (1oz) cocoa powder, sifted
75g (3oz) self-raising flour, sifted
3 large eggs, beaten
sifted cocoa powder to dust

**1** Preheat the oven to 170°C (150°C fan oven) mark 3. Grease a 20.5cm (8in) square, 5cm (2in) deep baking tin and base-line with baking parchment.

**2** Put the butter and chocolate into a heatproof bowl set over a pan of gently simmering water, making sure the base of the bowl doesn't touch the water. Stir until melted. Remove from the heat and stir in the sugar, vanilla extract, pecan nuts, cocoa, flour and eggs. Turn the mixture into the prepared tin and level the surface.

**3** Bake for about 1¼ hours or until set to the centre on the surface but still soft underneath. Leave to cool in the tin for 2 hours.

**4** Turn out, dust with sifted cocoa powder and cut into 16 individual brownies. Eat cold or serve warm with ice cream.

| Serves | EASY | | NUTRITIONAL INFORMATION |
|---|---|---|---|
| **16** | **Preparation Time** 15 minutes, plus cooling | **Cooking Time** 1 hour 20 minutes, plus cooling | **Per Brownie** 257 calories; 11g fat (of which 6g saturates); 38g carbohydrate; 0.2g salt |

## Freezing Tip

**To freeze** Complete the recipe to the end of step 4. Cool completely, keeping the cake in its greaseproof paper, then wrap in clingfilm. Freeze for up to one month.
**To use** Thaw overnight at cool room temperature. Complete the recipe.

275g (10oz) unsalted butter, softened, plus extra to grease

275g (10oz) golden caster sugar

400g (14oz) self-raising flour

1½ tsp baking powder

5 medium eggs, beaten

finely grated zest of 1 large orange

1 tbsp vanilla extract

4–5 tbsp milk

250g (9oz) blackberries

40g (1½oz) flaked almonds

# Blackberry Traybake

### ICING

150g (5oz) icing sugar

1 tsp vanilla extract

about 2 tbsp orange juice

**1** Preheat the oven to 190°C (170°C fan oven) mark 5. Grease a shallow 30.5 x 20.5cm (12 x 8in) baking tin and line with greaseproof paper.

**2** Put the butter and caster sugar into a large bowl. Sift in the flour and baking powder, then add the eggs, orange zest, vanilla extract and milk and beat together until light and fluffy.

**3** Using a metal spoon, fold in half the blackberries. Spoon into the prepared tin and dot with the remaining blackberries, then the almonds.

**4** Bake for 40–45 minutes until springy to the touch. Cool in the tin for 5 minutes, then turn out on to a wire rack and leave to cool completely.

**5** When the cake is cool, make the icing. Sift the icing sugar into a bowl, then add the vanilla extract and orange juice, mixing as you go, until smooth and runny. Drizzle over the cake and leave for 30 minutes to set. Cut into 24 squares to serve.

| EASY | | NUTRITIONAL INFORMATION | Serves |
|---|---|---|---|
| **Preparation Time**<br>20 minutes | **Cooking Time**<br>40–45 minutes, plus cooling and setting | **Per Square**<br>239 calories; 12g fat (of which 7g saturates);<br>32g carbohydrate; 0.4g salt | **24** |

# Carrot Traybake

100g (3½oz) unsalted butter, chopped, plus extra to grease

140g (4½oz) carrots, peeled and grated

100g (3½oz) sultanas

100g (3½oz) dried dates, chopped

50g (2oz) tenderised coconut

1 tsp ground cinnamon

½ tsp freshly grated nutmeg

1 x 330g bottle maple syrup

150ml (¼ pint) apple juice

grated zest and juice of 2 oranges

225g (8oz) wholemeal self-raising flour, sifted

2 tsp bicarbonate of soda

125g (4oz) walnut pieces

**TOPPING**

pared zest from ½–1 orange

200g (7oz) cream cheese

200g (7oz) crème fraîche

2 tbsp icing sugar

1 tsp vanilla extract

**1** Preheat the oven to 190°C (170°C fan oven) mark 5. Grease a 23cm (9in) square cake tin and line with greaseproof paper.

**2** Put the butter, carrots, sultanas, dates, coconut, spices, syrup, apple juice and orange zest and juice into a large pan. Cover and bring to the boil, then cook for 5 minutes. Tip into a bowl and leave to cool.

**3** Put the flour, bicarbonate of soda and walnuts into a large bowl and stir together. Add the cooled carrot mixture and stir well. Spoon the mixture into the prepared tin and level the surface.

**4** Bake for 45 minutes–1 hour until firm. Cool in the tin for 10 minutes, then turn out on to a wire rack and leave to cool completely.

**5** To make the topping, finely slice the orange zest and put to one side. Put the cream cheese, crème fraîche, icing sugar and vanilla extract into a bowl and stir with a spatula. Spread over the cake and top with the zest. Cut into 15 squares to serve.

| Serves | EASY | | NUTRITIONAL INFORMATION |
|---|---|---|---|
| **15** | **Preparation Time** 30 minutes | **Cooking Time** 50 minutes– 1 hour 5 minutes | **Per Square** 399 calories; 25g fat (of which 13g saturates); 41g carbohydrate; 0.4g salt |

# White Chocolate and Nut Brownies

75g (3oz) unsalted butter, plus extra to grease

500g (1lb 2oz) white chocolate, roughly chopped

3 large eggs

175g (6oz) golden caster sugar

175g (6oz) self-raising flour

pinch of salt

175g (6oz) macadamia nuts, roughly chopped

1 tsp vanilla extract

**1** Preheat the oven to 190°C (170°C fan oven) mark 5. Grease a 25.5 x 20.5cm (10 x 8in) baking tin and base-line with baking parchment.

**2** Melt 125g (4oz) white chocolate with the butter in a heatproof bowl set over a pan of gently simmering water, making sure the base of the bowl doesn't touch the water, stirring occasionally. Remove the bowl from the pan and leave to cool slightly.

**3** Whisk the eggs and sugar together in a large bowl until smooth, then gradually beat in the melted chocolate mixture – the consistency will become quite firm. Sift the flour and salt over the mixture, then fold in with the nuts, the remaining chopped chocolate and the vanilla extract. Turn the mixture into the prepared tin and level the surface.

**4** Bake for 30–35 minutes until risen and golden and the centre is just firm to the touch – the mixture will still be soft under the crust; it firms up on cooling. Leave to cool in the tin.

**5** Turn out and cut into 12 individual brownies.

| EASY | | NUTRITIONAL INFORMATION | Serves |
|---|---|---|---|
| **Preparation Time** 20 minutes | **Cooking Time** 35–40 minutes, plus cooling | **Per Brownie** 502 calories; 31g fat (of which 13g saturates); 52g carbohydrate; 0.4g salt | **12** |

# Chocolate Pecan Bars

125g (4oz) plain flour, sifted

25g (1oz) icing sugar

200g (7oz) unsalted butter, plus extra to grease

1 large egg yolk and 2 large eggs

125g (4oz) self-raising flour

1 tsp baking powder

125g (4oz) caster sugar

3–4 drops vanilla extract

150g (5oz) milk chocolate chips

75g (3oz) pecan nuts, chopped

6 tbsp chocolate and hazelnut spread

**1** Preheat the oven to 200°C (180°C fan oven) mark 6. Grease a 25.5 x 15cm (10 x 6in) shallow baking tin and base-line with baking parchment.

**2** Put the plain flour and icing sugar into a food processor with 75g (3oz) roughly chopped butter and whiz until crumb-like in texture. (Alternatively, rub the butter into the dry ingredients in a large bowl by hand or using a pastry blender.) Add the egg yolk and whiz for 10–15 seconds, or add to the bowl with the dry ingredients and stir until the mixture begins to come together. Turn into the tin and press into a thin layer. Bake for 15 minutes or until golden.

**3** Meanwhile, put the self-raising flour, baking powder, caster sugar, vanilla extract and the remaining eggs into the food processor with the remaining softened butter and blend for 15 seconds or until smooth (or put the ingredients into a bowl and mix well with a wooden spoon). Remove the blade and fold in the chocolate chips and pecan nuts. Set aside.

**4** Spread the chocolate and hazelnut spread over the cooked base and top with the cake mixture. Lower the oven setting to 180°C (160°C fan oven) mark 4 and bake for 45–50 minutes until golden – cover the top of the cake with foil if it appears to be browning too quickly. Cool in the tin for about 10 minutes, then turn out on to a wire rack and leave to cool completely. Cut into 25 pieces.

| Serves | EASY | | NUTRITIONAL INFORMATION |
|---|---|---|---|
| **25** | **Preparation Time** 15 minutes | **Cooking Time** 1 hour 5 minutes, plus cooling | **Per Bar** 189 calories; 13g fat (of which 6g saturates); 18g carbohydrate; 0.2g salt |

# Cherry Chocolate Fudge Brownies

150g (5oz) unsalted butter, plus extra to grease
200g (7oz) plain chocolate (at least 70% cocoa solids)
175g (6oz) caster sugar
2 tsp vanilla extract
5 medium eggs
175g (6oz) plain flour
3/4 tsp baking powder
250g (9oz) glacé cherries, halved

### ICING

150g (5oz) plain chocolate (at least 70% cocoa solids)
2 tbsp Kirsch
4 tbsp double cream

**1** Preheat the oven to 180°C (160°C fan oven) mark 4. Grease an 18cm (7in) square shallow cake tin and baseline with greaseproof paper. Put the butter and chocolate into a heatproof bowl set over a pan of gently simmering water, making sure the base of the bowl doesn't touch the water. Leave the chocolate to melt without stirring. Remove the bowl from the pan and stir until smooth. Leave to cool.

**2** Whisk the sugar, vanilla extract and eggs until pale and thick. Stir the chocolate into the egg mixture. Sift the flour and baking powder together and lightly fold into the mixture with the cherries. Pour the mixture into the prepared tin and bake for 40 minutes or until just set. Cool slightly in the tin before icing.

**3** To make the icing, put the chocolate and Kirsch into a heatproof bowl set over a pan of gently simmering water, making sure the base of the bowl doesn't touch the water. Once melted, add the cream and 4 tbsp water and stir well. Pour over the brownie and leave to set. Cut into 12 individual brownies.

| Serves 12 | EASY | | NUTRITIONAL INFORMATION |
|---|---|---|---|
| | **Preparation Time** 20 minutes | **Cooking Time** 50 minutes, plus cooling and setting | **Per Brownie** 462 calories; 24g fat (of which 14g saturates); 59g carbohydrate; 0.3g salt |

175g (6oz) unsalted butter, cut into pieces

150g (5oz) light muscovado sugar

2 tbsp golden syrup

375g (13oz) porridge oats

100g (3½oz) ready-to-eat dried papaya, roughly chopped

50g (2oz) sultanas

50g (2oz) pecan nuts, roughly chopped

25g (1oz) pinenuts

25g (1oz) pumpkin seeds

1 tbsp plain flour

1 tsp ground cinnamon

# Muesli Bars

**1** Preheat the oven to 180°C (160°C fan oven) mark 4. Melt the butter, sugar and syrup together in a heavy-based pan over a low heat.

**2** Meanwhile, put the oats, dried fruit, nuts, seeds, flour and cinnamon into a large bowl and stir to mix. Pour in the melted mixture and mix together until combined.

**3** Spoon the mixture into a 30.5 x 20.5cm (12 x 8in) non-stick baking tin and press down into the corners.

**4** Bake for 25–30 minutes until golden. Press the mixture down again if necessary, then use a palette knife to mark into 12 bars. Leave in the tin to cool completely.

**5** Use a palette knife to lift the bars out of the tin.

| EASY | | NUTRITIONAL INFORMATION | Serves |
|---|---|---|---|
| **Preparation Time** 10 minutes, plus cooling | **Cooking Time** 30–35 minutes, plus cooling | **Per Bar** 386 calories; 21g fat (of which 8g saturates); 48g carbohydrate; 0.3g salt | **12** |

50ml (2fl oz) sunflower oil, plus extra to grease

250g (9oz) plain chocolate (at least 50% cocoa solids)

4 medium eggs

150g (5oz) light muscovado sugar

1 tsp vanilla extract

75g (3oz) plain flour

¼ tsp baking powder

1 tbsp cocoa powder

# Low-fat Brownies

**1** Preheat the oven to 200°C (180°C fan oven) mark 6. Grease a 20.5cm (8in) square shallow tin and base-line with baking parchment.

**2** Melt the chocolate in a heatproof bowl set over a pan of gently simmering water, making sure the base of the bowl doesn't touch the water. Remove the bowl from the pan and put to one side to cool slightly.

**3** Put the eggs into a large bowl, add the oil, sugar and vanilla extract and whisk together until pale and thick. Sift the flour, baking powder and cocoa powder into the bowl, then carefully pour in the chocolate. Using a large metal spoon, gently fold all the ingredients together – if you fold too roughly, the chocolate will seize up and become unusable.

**4** Carefully pour the brownie mixture into the prepared tin and bake for 20 minutes – when cooked, the brownie should be fudgy inside and the top should be cracked and crispy. Cut into 16 individual brownies immediately, then leave to cool in the tin.

| Serves | EASY | | NUTRITIONAL INFORMATION |
|---|---|---|---|
| **16** | **Preparation Time**<br>10 minutes | **Cooking Time**<br>25 minutes,<br>plus cooling | **Per Brownie**<br>172 calories; 8g fat (of which 3g saturates);<br>24g carbohydrate; 0.1g salt |

# Apricot and Almond Traybake

250g (9oz) unsalted butter, softened, plus extra to grease

225g (8oz) golden caster sugar

275g (10oz) self-raising flour, sifted

2 tsp baking powder

finely grated zest of 1 orange and 2 tbsp orange juice

75g (3oz) ground almonds

5 medium eggs, lightly beaten

225g (8oz) ready-to-eat dried apricots, roughly chopped

25g (1oz) flaked almonds

icing sugar to dust (optional)

**1** Preheat the oven to 180°C (160°C fan oven) mark 4. Grease a 33 x 20.5cm (13 x 8in) baking tin and base-line with baking parchment.

**2** Put the butter, caster sugar, flour, baking powder, orange zest, ground almonds and eggs into the bowl of a large freestanding mixer. Mix on a low setting for 30 seconds, then increase the speed and mix for 1 minute or until thoroughly combined. (Alternatively, mix well, using a wooden spoon.)

**3** Remove the bowl from the mixer. Using a large metal spoon, fold in the apricots. Spoon the mixture into the prepared tin, level the surface and sprinkle the flaked almonds over the top.

**4** Bake for 30–40 minutes until risen and golden brown and a skewer inserted into the centre comes out clean. Leave to cool in the tin.

**5** Cut into 18 bars. Dust with icing sugar, if you like.

| EASY | | NUTRITIONAL INFORMATION | Serves |
| --- | --- | --- | --- |
| **Preparation Time**<br>20 minutes | **Cooking Time**<br>30–40 minutes,<br>plus cooling | **Per Bar**<br>277 calories; 16g fat (of which 8g saturates);<br>30g carbohydrate; 0.4g salt | **18** |

# Quick Chocolate Slices

225g (8oz) unsalted butter or olive oil spread
50g (2oz) cocoa powder, sifted
3 tbsp golden syrup
1 x 300g pack digestive biscuits, crushed
400g (14oz) plain chocolate (at least 70% cocoa solids),
broken into pieces

**1** Put the butter or olive oil spread into a heatproof bowl, add the cocoa powder and syrup and melt over a pan of gently simmering water. Mix everything together.

**2** Remove from the heat and stir in the biscuits. Mix well until thoroughly coated in chocolate, crushing any large pieces of biscuit. Turn into a greased 25.5 x 16.5cm (10 x 6½in) tin and leave to cool, then cover and chill for 20 minutes.

**3** Melt the chocolate in a heatproof bowl in a 900W microwave oven on full power for 1 minute 40 seconds, stirring twice. (Alternatively, put into a heatproof bowl set over a pan of gently simmering water, making sure the base of the bowl doesn't touch the water.) Stir once more and pour over the chocolate biscuit base, then chill for 20 minutes.

**4** Cut in half lengthways. Cut each half into 20 rectangular slices.

| Serves | EASY | | NUTRITIONAL INFORMATION |
|---|---|---|---|
| **40** | **Preparation Time** 10 minutes | **Cooking Time** 5–10 minutes, plus chilling | **Per Slice** 137 calories; 9g fat (of which 6g saturates); 13g carbohydrate; 0.3g salt |

## Note

----------------------------------------------------

If not serving straightaway, wrap in baking parchment, tie up with string and store in the fridge. It will keep for up to four weeks – unwrap and drizzle with 1 tsp brandy every week.

500g (1lb 2oz) ready-to-eat dried figs, hard stalks removed

50g (2oz) candied orange peel, finely chopped

75g (3oz) hazelnuts, toasted

50g (2oz) shelled pistachio nuts

50g (2oz) plain chocolate, broken into pieces

50g (2oz) ready-to-eat pitted dates

¼ tsp ground cinnamon

pinch of freshly grated nutmeg

4 tbsp brandy, plus extra to drizzle

rice paper

# Figgy Fruit Slice

**1** Put the figs and candied orange peel into a food processor and whiz for 1 minute to mince the fruit finely. Tip into a large bowl.

**2** Put the hazelnuts, pistachio nuts, chocolate and dates into the food processor with the spices and 4 tbsp brandy and pulse to chop roughly. Add to the fig mixture and mix, using your hands.

**3** Put a sheet of rice paper on a baking sheet. Spoon the fig mixture evenly on top, then press down with the back of a wet spoon to form an even layer about 2cm (¾in) thick. Put another sheet of rice paper on top and press down well. Chill for 1 hour.

**4** Cut the slice into four rectangles to serve.

| EASY | | NUTRITIONAL INFORMATION | Serves |
|---|---|---|---|
| **Preparation Time** 30 minutes, plus chilling | **Cooking Time** None | **Per Slice** 577 calories, 20g fat (of which 4g saturates), 86g carbohydrate, 0.4g salt | **4** |

## Cook's Tip

If, towards the end of coating the cakes, the chocolate topping mixture has thickened, carefully stir in a drop of water to thin it down.

# Lamingtons

125g (4oz) unsalted butter, softened, plus extra to grease

125g (4oz) golden caster sugar

2 medium eggs

125g (4oz) self-raising flour, sifted

1 tsp baking powder

2 tsp vanilla extract

### COATING

200g (7oz) icing sugar

50g (2oz) cocoa powder

25g (1oz) unsalted butter, cubed

5 tbsp milk

200g (7oz) desiccated coconut

**1** Preheat the oven to 180°C (160°C fan oven) mark 4. Grease a 15cm (6in) square cake tin and base-line with baking parchment.

**2** Put the butter, caster sugar, eggs, flour, baking powder and vanilla extract into a bowl and beat with a hand-held electric whisk until creamy. Turn the mixture into the prepared tin and level the surface. Bake for about 30 minutes or until just firm to the touch and a skewer inserted into the centre comes out clean. Transfer to a wire rack to cool completely. Wrap and store, preferably overnight, so that the cake is easier to slice.

**3** To make the coating, sift the icing sugar and cocoa powder into a bowl. Put the butter and milk into a small pan and heat until the butter has just melted. Pour over the icing sugar and stir until smooth, adding 2–3 tbsp water if necessary, so that the icing thickly coats the back of a spoon.

**4** Trim the side crusts from the cake and cut into 16 squares. Place a sheet of greaseproof paper under a wire rack to catch the drips. Scatter the coconut on to a large plate. Pierce a piece of cake through the top crust and dip into the icing until coated, turning the cake gently. Transfer to the wire rack. Once you've coated half the pieces, roll them in the coconut and transfer to a plate. Repeat with the remainder and leave to set for a couple of hours before serving.

| Serves | EASY | | NUTRITIONAL INFORMATION |
|---|---|---|---|
| **16** | **Preparation Time** 40 minutes | **Cooking Time** 35 minutes, plus cooling and setting | **Per Square** 273 calories; 17g fat (of which 12g saturates); 29g carbohydrate; 0.4g salt |

# Chocolate Fudge Brownies

butter to grease

125g (4oz) milk chocolate

9 ready-to-eat dried prunes

200g (7oz) light muscovado sugar

3 large egg whites

1 tsp vanilla extract

75g (3oz) plain flour, sifted

50g (2oz) white chocolate, chopped

icing sugar to dust

**1** Preheat the oven to 180°C (160°C fan oven) mark 4. Grease a 15cm (6in) square shallow cake tin and base-line with baking parchment.

**2** Melt the milk chocolate in a heatproof bowl set over a pan of gently simmering water, making sure the base of the bowl doesn't touch the water. Remove from the heat and leave to cool slightly.

**3** Put the prunes into a food processor or blender with 100ml (3½fl oz) water and whiz for 2–3 minutes to make a purée. Add the muscovado sugar and whiz briefly to mix.

**4** Put the egg whites into a clean, grease-free bowl and whisk until soft peaks form.

**5** Add the vanilla extract, prune mixture, flour, white chocolate and egg whites to the bowl of melted chocolate and fold everything together gently. Pour the mixture into the prepared tin and bake for 1 hour or until firm to the touch.

**6** Leave to cool in the tin. Turn out, dust with icing sugar and cut into 12 individual brownies.

| **EASY** | | **NUTRITIONAL INFORMATION** | **Serves** |
|---|---|---|---|
| **Preparation Time** 20 minutes | **Cooking Time** 1 hour 5 minutes, plus cooling | **Per Brownie** 174 calories; 5g fat (of which 3g saturates); 33g carbohydrate; 0.1g salt | **12** |

# Hazelnut and Chocolate Flapjacks

125g (4oz) unsalted butter, plus extra to grease

125g (4oz) light muscovado sugar

1 tbsp golden syrup

50g (2oz) hazelnuts, roughly chopped

175g (6oz) jumbo or porridge oats

50g (2oz) plain chocolate such as Bournville, roughly chopped

**1** Preheat the oven to 180°C (160°C fan oven) mark 4. Lightly grease a shallow 28 x 18cm (11 x 7in) baking tin.

**2** Put the butter, sugar and syrup into a pan and melt together over a low heat. Stir in the hazelnuts and oats. Leave the mixture to cool slightly, then stir in the chocolate. Spoon the mixture into the prepared tin and level the surface.

**3** Bake for about 30 minutes until golden and firm. Cool in the tin for a few minutes, then cut into 12 pieces. Turn out on to a wire rack and leave to cool completely.

## Try Something Different

- - - - - - - - - - - - - - - - - - - - - - - - - - - - - - - - - - - - - -

**Tropical Fruit and Coconut Flapjacks:** Replace the hazelnuts and chocolate with mixed dried tropical fruits, chopped into pieces. Replace 50g (2oz) of the oats with desiccated coconut.

**Apricot and Mixed Seed Flapjacks:** Replace the hazelnuts with 50g (2oz) mixed seeds (such as pumpkin, sunflower, linseed and sesame). Reduce the oats to 125g (4oz) and replace the chocolate with 100g (3¹/₂oz) chopped dried apricots.

| EASY | | NUTRITIONAL INFORMATION | Serves |
|---|---|---|---|
| **Preparation Time** 10 minutes | **Cooking Time** 35 minutes, plus cooling | **Per Flapjack** 229 calories; 14g fat (of which 6g saturates); 26g carbohydrate; 0.2g salt | **12** |

**Note**

Don't overcook the flapjacks or they will be hard and dry.
When they are cooked, they should still be sticky and
slightly soft when you press them in the middle.

# Sticky Ginger Flapjacks

350g (12oz) unsalted butter, plus extra to grease

275g (10oz) caster sugar

225g (8oz) golden syrup

450g (1lb) rolled oats

1 tbsp ground ginger

**1** Preheat the oven to 180°C (160°C fan oven) mark 4.
Grease a 28 x 18cm (11 x 7in) shallow cake tin and
base-line with baking parchment.

**2** Put the butter, sugar and syrup into a large pan and
heat gently until melted. Mix in the rolled oats and
ground ginger until they are thoroughly combined.
Pour the mixture into the tin and level the surface.

**3** Bake for 30–35 minutes until golden brown around
the edges. Leave to cool in the tin for 15 minutes.

**4** While still warm, score into 24 pieces with a sharp
knife. Leave in the tin to cool completely, then turn
out and cut out the pieces.

| Serves | EASY | | NUTRITIONAL INFORMATION |
|---|---|---|---|
| **24** | **Preparation Time**<br>10 minutes | **Cooking Time**<br>40 minutes,<br>plus cooling | **Per Flapjack**<br>259 calories; 14g fat (of which 8g saturates);<br>33g carbohydrate; 0.3g salt |

## Cook's Tip

Don't worry if your baking tin is not the exact size; use one of similar dimensions.

## Try Something Different

Instead of mixed dried fruit, use chopped dried apricots.

# Fruit and Nut Flapjack

250g (9oz) unsalted butter, cut into pieces, plus extra to grease

250g (9oz) caster sugar

175g (6oz) golden syrup

425g (15oz) rolled oats

125g (4oz) mixed dried fruit, including glacé cherries

75g (3oz) chopped nuts, toasted

**1** Preheat the oven to 180°C (160°C fan oven) mark 4. Grease a shallow 28 x 20.5cm (11 x 8in) baking tin.

**2** Put the butter, sugar and syrup into a large heavy-based pan. Stir over a moderate heat until the butter has melted. Remove from the heat and stir in the oats, dried fruit and nuts. Turn into the prepared tin and level the surface.

**3** Bake for 25–30 minutes until deep golden around the edges; the mixture will still be very soft in the middle. Leave in the tin until almost cold. Remove from the tin and cut into 36 squares.

| EASY | | NUTRITIONAL INFORMATION | Serves |
|---|---|---|---|
| **Preparation Time** 10 minutes | **Cooking Time** 30–35 minutes, plus cooling | **Per Flapjack** 162 calories, 8g fat (of which 4g saturates), 22g carbohydrate, 0.2g salt | **36** |

# Raspberry and Cream Cheese Chocolate Brownies

200g (7oz) unsalted butter, plus extra to grease

300g (10oz) plain chocolate (at least 70% cocoa solids), chopped

4 medium eggs

150g (5oz) light muscovado sugar

125g (4oz) plus 1 tbsp self-raising flour, sifted

125g (4oz) curd cheese or cream cheese

2 tbsp raspberry jam

crème fraîche to serve

**1** Preheat the oven to 200°C (180°C fan oven) mark 6. Grease a 23cm (9in) square tin and line with greaseproof paper. Put both chocolates and the butter into a heatproof bowl set over a pan of simmering water and stir to combine. When they have melted, take off the heat and set aside to cool.

**2** Put 3 of the eggs and all but 1 tsp sugar into a bowl and whisk together with a hand-held electric whisk until thick and mousse-like. Fold in the cooled chocolate mixture and all but the 1 tbsp flour, then pour into the prepared tin.

**3** Put the cheese into a bowl with the remaining egg and the reserved 1 tsp sugar and 1 tbsp flour. Mix well to combine.

**4** Place dollops of the cheese mixture randomly over the surface, then top each with 1 tsp of the raspberry jam. Use a skewer to marble the cheese, jam and brownie mixture together.

**5** Bake for 25–30 minutes. Remove from the oven and cool in the tin for 10 minutes, then turn out on to a wire rack and leave to cool completely. Cut into 9 individual brownies and serve with a dollop of crème fraîche.

| Serves | EASY | | NUTRITIONAL INFORMATION |
|---|---|---|---|
| **9** | **Preparation Time** 20 minutes, plus cooling | **Cooking Time** about 35 minutes, plus cooling | **Per Brownie** 465 calories; 32g fat (of which 20g saturates); 41g carbohydrate; 0.7g salt |

## Try Something Different

------------------------------------------------------------

**Cherry and Coconut Crumble Bars:** Rinse and dry 225g (8oz) glacé cherries and quarter them; fold the cherries into the crumble topping at the end of step 2. Make the sponge base as in step 3, adding 50g (2oz) desiccated coconut to the ingredients.

250g (9oz) unsalted butter, softened, plus extra to grease

250g (9oz) caster sugar

125g (4oz) plain flour, sifted

175g (6oz) self-raising flour

grated zest of 1 lemon

3 large eggs

1½ tsp vanilla extract

# Vanilla Crumble Bars

**1** Preheat the oven to 180°C (160°C fan oven) mark 4. Grease a 25.5 x 18cm (10 x 7in) shallow baking tin and base-line with baking parchment.

**2** To make the crumble topping, put 75g (3oz) butter and 75g (3oz) sugar into a food processor and whiz until smooth. Add the plain flour and whiz for 8–10 seconds until the mixture forms very rough breadcrumbs, then put to one side.

**3** Put the remaining butter and sugar, the self-raising flour, lemon zest, eggs and vanilla extract into the food processor and whiz for about 15 seconds or until smooth. Pour the mixture into the prepared tin, sprinkle the crumble topping over the surface and press down to cover.

**4** Bake for 50–60 minutes (if necessary, cover loosely with foil for the last 10 minutes if the top is browning too quickly). Leave to cool in the tin for 5 minutes. Turn out on to a wire rack and cut into 25 bars.

| EASY | | NUTRITIONAL INFORMATION | Serves |
|---|---|---|---|
| **Preparation Time** 15 minutes | **Cooking Time** 50–60 minutes, plus cooling | **Per Bar** 295 calories; 10g fat (of which 5g saturates); 50g carbohydrate; 0.6g salt | **25** |

# 4

# **Biscuits and Cookies**

Chocolate Chip Oat Cookies

Sultana and Pecan Cookies

Peanut and Raisin Cookies

Almond Cookies

White and Dark Chocolate Cookies

Orange Tuile Biscuits

Florentines

## Freezing Tip

**To freeze** Complete the recipe and allow the cookies to cool. Wrap, seal, label and freeze.
**To use** Thaw the cookies individually, as needed, at room temperature for 1–2 hours.

# Chocolate Chip Oat Cookies

125g (4oz) unsalted butter, softened, plus extra to grease

125g (4oz) golden caster sugar

1 medium egg

1 tsp vanilla extract

125g (4oz) porridge oats

150g (5oz) plain flour

$\frac{1}{2}$ tsp baking powder

200g (7oz) plain chocolate (at least 70% cocoa solids), cut into 1cm ($\frac{1}{2}$in) chunks

**1** Preheat the oven to 180°C (160°C fan oven) mark 4. Lightly grease two baking sheets.

**2** Cream the butter and sugar together in a bowl until pale and creamy. Add the egg, vanilla extract and oats. Sift the flour and baking powder together over the mixture and mix until evenly combined. Stir in the chocolate chunks.

**3** Put dessertspoonfuls of the mixture on to the prepared baking sheets, spacing them well apart to allow room for spreading. Flatten each one slightly with the back of a fork.

**4** Bake for 12–15 minutes until risen and turning golden, but still quite soft. Leave on the baking sheet for 5 minutes, then transfer to a wire rack to cool completely.

| Serves | EASY | | NUTRITIONAL INFORMATION |
|---|---|---|---|
| **18** | **Preparation Time** 15 minutes | **Cooking Time** 12–15 minutes, plus cooling | **Per Cookie** 197 calories; 10g fat (of which 6g saturates); 26g carbohydrate; 0.2g salt |

**Freezing Tip**

**To freeze** Complete the recipe to the end of step 4, then open-freeze a tray of unbaked cookies. When frozen, pack into bags or containers.
**To use** Cook from frozen for 18–20 minutes.

# Sultana and Pecan Cookies

225g (8oz) unsalted butter, at room temperature, plus extra to grease

175g (6oz) light muscovado sugar

2 medium eggs, lightly beaten

225g (8oz) pecan nut halves

300g (11oz) self-raising flour, sifted

¼ tsp baking powder

125g (4oz) sultanas

2 tbsp maple syrup

**1** Preheat the oven to 190°C (170°C fan oven) mark 5. Lightly grease four baking sheets.

**2** Cream the butter and sugar together until the mixture is pale and fluffy. Gradually beat in the eggs until thoroughly combined.

**3** Put 20 pecan nut halves to one side, then roughly chop the rest and fold into the mixture with the flour, baking powder, sultanas and syrup.

**4** Roll the mixture into 20 balls and place them, spaced well apart, on to the prepared baking sheets. Using a dampened palette knife, flatten the cookies and top each with a piece of pecan nut.

**5** Bake for 12–15 minutes until pale golden. Leave on the baking sheets for 5 minutes, then transfer to a wire rack to cool completely.

| EASY | | NUTRITIONAL INFORMATION | Serves |
|---|---|---|---|
| **Preparation Time** 15 minutes | **Cooking Time** 12–15 minutes, plus cooling | **Per Cookie** 276 calories; 18g fat (of which 7g saturates); 27g carbohydrate; 0.2g salt | **20** |

## Try Something Different

**Chocolate Walnut Cookies:** Omit the peanut butter and raisins and add 1 tsp vanilla extract. Stir in 175g (6oz) roughly chopped chocolate and 75g (3oz) roughly chopped walnuts.

**Coconut and Cherry Cookies:** Omit the peanut butter and raisins, reduce the sugar to 75g (3oz) and stir in 50g (2oz) desiccated coconut and 125g (4oz) rinsed, roughly chopped glacé cherries.

**Oat and Cinnamon Cookies:** Omit the peanut butter and raisins and add 1 tsp vanilla extract. Stir in 1 tsp ground cinnamon and 75g (3oz) rolled oats.

# Peanut and Raisin Cookies

125g (4oz) unsalted butter, softened, plus extra to grease
150g (5oz) caster sugar
1 medium egg
150g (5oz) plain flour, sifted
½ tsp baking powder
½ tsp salt
125g (4oz) crunchy peanut butter
175g (6oz) raisins

**1** Preheat the oven to 190°C (170°C fan oven) mark 5 and grease two baking sheets. Beat together all the ingredients except the raisins, until well blended. Stir in the raisins.

**2** Spoon large teaspoonfuls of the mixture, spaced well apart, on to the prepared baking sheets, leaving room for the mixture to spread.

**3** Bake for about 15 minutes or until golden brown around the edges. Leave to cool slightly, then transfer to a wire rack to cool completely.

| Serves | EASY | | NUTRITIONAL INFORMATION |
|---|---|---|---|
| **30** | **Preparation Time** 10 minutes | **Cooking Time** 15 minutes, plus cooling | **Per Cookie** 111 calories; 6g fat (of which 3g saturates); 14g carbohydrate; 0.2g salt |

**Try Something Different**

Instead of a glacé cherry, use whole almonds or a sprinkling of lemon zest to top each cookie.

2 medium egg whites

200g (7oz) caster sugar

200g (7oz) ground almonds

grated zest of 1 orange

$\frac{1}{2}$ tsp ground ginger

40g (1$\frac{1}{2}$oz) stem ginger in syrup, drained and roughly chopped

2 tbsp plain flour, sifted, to dust

12 natural glacé cherries

rice paper for lining

# Almond Cookies

**1** Preheat the oven to 180°C (160°C fan oven) mark 4. Line two baking sheets with rice paper. Put the egg whites into a large, clean, grease-free bowl and whisk until they form stiff peaks. In another large bowl, stir the sugar, ground almonds, orange zest, $\frac{1}{4}$ tsp ground ginger and the stem ginger together. With a wooden spoon, mix in the egg whites to form a sticky dough.

**2** Roll the dough into 12 equal-sized balls. Mix the flour and remaining ground ginger together in a bowl. Lightly coat each ball in the flour and shake off the excess. Put the balls, spaced well apart, on to the prepared baking sheets. Using a dampened palette knife, flatten each one into a round.

**3** Push a glacé cherry into the middle of each cookie and bake for 15–20 minutes until lightly golden. Cool on a wire rack, then trim away the excess rice paper.

| EASY | | NUTRITIONAL INFORMATION | Serves |
|---|---|---|---|
| **Preparation Time** 15 minutes | **Cooking Time** 15–20 minutes, plus cooling | **Per Cookie** 204 calories; 10g fat (of which 1g saturates); 27g carbohydrate; 0g salt | **12** |

# White and Dark Chocolate Cookies

125g (4oz) unsalted butter, softened, plus extra to grease

125g (4oz) golden caster sugar

2 medium eggs, beaten

2 tsp vanilla extract

250g (9oz) self-raising flour, sifted

finely grated zest of 1 orange

100g (3½oz) white chocolate, roughly chopped

100g (3½oz) plain chocolate (at least 70% cocoa solids), roughly chopped

**1** Preheat the oven to 180°C (160°C fan oven) mark 4. Lightly grease three baking sheets.

**2** Cream the butter and sugar together until the mixture is pale and fluffy. Gradually beat in the eggs and vanilla extract. Sift in the flour, then add the orange zest and sprinkle in the white and plain chocolate. Mix the dough together with your hands. Knead lightly, then wrap in clingfilm and chill for at least 30 minutes.

**3** Divide the mixture into 26 pieces and roll each into a ball. Using a dampened palette knife, flatten each ball slightly to make a disc, then put on the prepared baking sheets, spaced well apart.

**4** Bake for about 10–12 minutes until golden. Leave on the baking sheets for 5 minutes, then transfer to a wire rack to cool completely.

| Serves | EASY | | NUTRITIONAL INFORMATION |
|---|---|---|---|
| **26** | **Preparation Time** 15 minutes, plus chilling | **Cooking Time** 10–12 minutes, plus cooling | **Per Cookie** 133 calories; 7g fat (of which 4g saturates); 17g carbohydrate; 0.1g salt |

# Orange Tuile Biscuits

3 large egg whites
100g (3½oz) icing sugar, sifted
100g (3½oz) plain flour
finely grated zest of 1 orange
75g (3oz) unsalted butter, melted

**1** Put the egg whites into a clean, grease-free bowl and lightly whisk with the sugar. Stir in the flour, orange zest and melted butter, then cover and chill for 30 minutes.

**2** Preheat the oven to 200°C (180°C fan oven) mark 6. Line a baking sheet with baking parchment.

**3** Put heaps of the mixture, of 3 tsp each, spaced well apart, on the prepared baking sheet and spread out into 9cm (3½in) circles.

**4** Bake for 12 minutes or until just brown around the edges. Remove from the oven and, while still warm, shape each biscuit over a rolling pin to curl. Repeat with the remaining mixture. Leave on a wire rack to cool completely.

| **EASY** | | **NUTRITIONAL INFORMATION** | **Serves** |
|---|---|---|---|
| **Preparation Time** 10 minutes, plus chilling | **Cooking Time** 12 minutes, plus cooling | **Per Biscuit** 55 calories; 3g fat (of which 2g saturates); 8g carbohydrate; 0.1g salt | **24** |

# Florentines

65g (2½oz) unsalted butter, plus extra to grease

50g (2oz) golden caster sugar

2 tbsp double cream

25g (1oz) sunflower seeds

20g (¾oz) chopped mixed candied peel

20g (¾oz) sultanas

25g (1oz) natural glacé cherries, roughly chopped

40g (1½oz) flaked almonds, lightly crushed

15g (½oz) plain flour

125g (4oz) plain chocolate (at least 70% cocoa solids),
broken into pieces

**1** Preheat the oven to 180°C (160°C fan oven) mark 4. Lightly grease two large baking sheets.

**2** Melt the butter in a small heavy-based pan. Add the sugar and heat gently until dissolved, then bring to the boil. Take off the heat and stir in the cream, seeds, peel, sultanas, cherries, almonds and flour. Mix until evenly combined. Put heaps, of 1 tsp each, on to the prepared baking sheets, spaced well apart to allow for spreading.

**3** Bake one sheet at a time, for 6–8 minutes, until the biscuits have spread considerably and the edges are golden brown. Using a large plain metal biscuit cutter, push the edges into the centre to create neat rounds. Bake for a further 2 minutes or until deep golden. Leave on the baking sheet for 2 minutes, then transfer to a wire rack to cool completely.

**4** Melt the chocolate in a heatproof bowl set over a pan of gently simmering water, making sure the base of the bowl doesn't touch the water, and stirring occasionally. Spread on the underside of each Florentine and mark wavy lines with a fork. Put, chocolate side up, on a sheet of baking parchment and leave to set.

| Serves | EASY | | NUTRITIONAL INFORMATION |
|---|---|---|---|
| **18** | **Preparation Time**<br>15 minutes | **Cooking Time**<br>16–18 minutes,<br>plus cooling | **Per Biscuit**<br>115 calories; 8g fat (of which 4g saturates);<br>11g carbohydrate; 0.1g salt |

# Glossary

**Al dente** Italian term commonly used to describe foods, especially pasta and vegetables, which are cooked until tender but still firm to the bite.

**Bain-marie** Literally, a water bath, used to keep foods, such as delicate custards and sauces, at a constant low temperature during cooking, or to melt chocolate. On the hob a double saucepan or bowl set over a pan of simmering water is used; for oven cooking, the baking dish(es) is placed in a roasting tin containing enough hot water to come halfway up the sides.

**Baking blind** Pre-baking a pastry case before filling. The pastry case is lined with greaseproof paper and weighted down with dried beans or ceramic baking beans.

**Baking powder** A raising agent consisting of an acid, usually cream of tartar and an alkali, such as bicarbonate of soda, which react to produce carbon dioxide. This expands during baking and makes cakes and breads rise.

**Beat** To incorporate air into an ingredient or mixture by agitating it vigorously with a spoon, fork, whisk or electric mixer. The technique is also used to soften ingredients.

**Bind** To mix beaten egg or other liquid into a dry mixture to hold it together.

**Blanch** To immerse food, such as peaches, nuts or tomatoes, briefly in fast-boiling water to loosen skins or to remove bitterness.

**Buttercream** A soft icing used to cover and fill cakes, made by creaming together butter and sugar.

**Caramelise** To heat sugar or sugar syrup slowly until it is brown in colour; ie forms a caramel.

**Chill** To cool food in the refrigerator.

**Compote** Fresh or dried fruit stewed in sugar syrup. Served hot or cold.

**Consistency** Term used to describe the texture of a mixture, eg firm, dropping or soft.

**Coulis** A smooth fruit or vegetable purée, thinned if necessary to a pouring consistency.

**Cream** To beat together fat and sugar until the mixture is pale and fluffy, and resembles whipped cream in texture and colour. The method is used in cakes and puddings that contain a high proportion of fat and require the incorporation of a lot of air.

**Crimp** To decorate the edge of a pie, tart or shortbread by pinching it at regular intervals to give a fluted effect.

**Curdle** To cause sauces or creamed mixtures to separate, usually by overheating or over-beating.

**Dice** To cut food into small cubes.

**Dredge** To sprinkle food generously with flour, sugar, icing sugar etc.

**Dust** To sprinkle lightly with flour, cornflour, icing sugar etc.

**Extract** Concentrated flavouring, which is used in small quantities, eg yeast extract, vanilla extract.

**Folding in** Method of combining a whisked or creamed mixture with other ingredients by cutting and folding so that it retains its lightness. A large metal spoon or plastic-bladed spatula is used.

**Frosting** To coat leaves and flowers with a fine layer of sugar to use as a decoration. Also an American term for icing cakes.

**Ganache** A rich filling or coating for cakes, choux buns and biscuits, made from chocolate and double cream.

**Glaze** A glossy coating given to sweet and savoury dishes to improve their appearance and sometimes flavour. Beaten egg, egg white or milk may be used to glaze pastry.

**Gluten** A protein constituent of grains, such as wheat and rye, which develops when the flour is mixed with water to give the dough elasticity.

**Hull** To remove the stalk and calyx from soft fruits such as strawberries.

**Infuse** To immerse flavourings, such as aromatic vegetables, herbs, spices or vanilla, in a liquid to impart flavour. Usually the infused liquid is brought to the boil, then left to stand for a while.

**Macerate** To soften and flavour raw or dried foods by soaking in a liquid, eg soaking fruit in alcohol.

**Madeleine tray** A baking tin with 12 shell-shaped indentations for baking traditional French madeleines.

**Mince** To cut food into very fine pieces, using a mincer, food processor or knife.

**Mocha** Term which has come to mean a blend of chocolate and coffee.

**Muffin case** Paper casing for cooking cupcakes and muffins.

**Muffin tin** Tray of cup-shaped moulds for cooking small cakes and deep tartlets. Also called a bun tin.

**Parboil** To boil a vegetable or other food for part of its cooking time before finishing it by another method.

**Pare** To finely peel the skin or zest from vegetables or fruit.

**Poach** To cook food gently in liquid at simmering point; the surface should be just trembling.

**Purée** To pound, sieve or liquidise vegetables, fish or fruit to a smooth pulp. Purées often form the basis for soups and sauces.

**Reduce** To fast-boil stock or other liquid in an uncovered pan to evaporate water and concentrate the flavour.

**Roast** To cook food by dry heat in the oven.

**Rubbing in** Method of incorporating fat into flour by rubbing between the fingertips; used when a short texture is required. Used for pastry, cakes, scones and biscuits.

**Sauté** To cook food in a small quantity of fat over a high heat, shaking the pan constantly – usually in a sauté pan (a frying pan with straight sides).

**Scald** To pour boiling water over food to clean it, or loosen skin, eg tomatoes. Also used to describe heating milk to just below boiling point.

**Score** To cut parallel lines in the surface of food, such as fish (or the fat layer on meat), to improve its appearance or help it cook more quickly.

**Shred** To grate cheese or slice vegetables or citrus zest into very fine pieces or strips.

**Sieve** To press food through a sieve to obtain a smooth texture.

**Sift** To shake dry ingredients through a sieve to remove lumps.

**Simmer** To keep a liquid just below boiling point.

**Steam** To cook food in steam, usually in a steamer over rapidly boiling water.

**Steep** To immerse food in warm or cold liquid to soften it, and sometimes to draw out strong flavours.

**Suet** Hard fat of animal origin used in pastry and steamed puddings. A vegetarian alternative is readily available.

**Sugar syrup** A concentrated solution of sugar in water used to poach fruit and make sorbets, granitas, fruit juices, and so on.

**Swiss roll tin** Shallow, rectangular tin, available in several different sizes, used for baking sponges that are filled and rolled after baking – such as roulades.

**Tepid** The term used to describe a temperature of approximately blood heat, ie 37°C (98.7°F).

**Vanilla sugar** Sugar in which a vanilla pod has been stored to impart its flavour.

**Whipping, whisking** Beating air rapidly into a mixture with either a manual or electric whisk. Whipping usually refers to cream.

**Zest** The thin, coloured outer layer of citrus fruit, which can be removed in fine strips with a zester.

# Index

**A**

all-in-one method 17
almonds: almond cookies 123
apricot and almond traybake 107
cherry and almond muffins 85
cherry Bakewell cupcakes 46
gluten-free pistachio and polenta cupcakes 59
aniseed cupcakes 72
apples 25
apple and cinnamon muffins 84
apple crumble cupcakes 48
apple madeleines 93
bran and apple muffins 80
apricots: apricot and almond traybake 107
apricot and mixed seed flapjacks 113

**B**

bakeware 11
Bakewell cupcakes 46
bananas: banoffee cupcakes 73
chocolate banana muffins 88
red nose buns 56
wholemeal banana muffins 83
banoffee cupcakes 73
be mine cupcakes 53
biscuits 18
orange tuile 125
rolled vanilla 19
blackberry traybake 99
blanching nuts 22
blueberries: blueberry muffins 81
Pavlova cupcakes 44
bowls 11
bran and apple muffins 80
Brazil nut and clementine cakes 90
breakfast cupcakes 61
brown sugar muffins 84
brownies: cherry chocolate fudge 104
chocolate fudge 111
double-chocolate 97
low-fat 106
raspberry and cream cheese chocolate 116
the ultimate chocolate 98
white chocolate and nut 101
buns, red nose 56
buttercream 27
butterfly cakes, chocolate 92

**C**

carrots: carrot traybake 100
spiced carrot muffins 86
the ultimate carrot cupcake 52
cherries: cherry and almond muffins 85
cherry and coconut crumble bars 117
cherry Bakewell cupcakes 46
cherry chocolate fudge brownies 104
coconut and cherry cookies 122
red nose buns 56
sour cherry cupcakes 37
chocolate 20–21
buttercream 27
cherry chocolate fudge brownies 104
chocolate banana muffins 88
chocolate butterfly cakes 92
chocolate chip oat cookies 120
chocolate cupcakes 32
chocolate fairy cakes 33
chocolate fudge brownies 111
chocolate nut cookies 122
chocolate pecan bars 102
double-chocolate brownies 97
double chocolate chip muffins 81
Easter cupcakes 65
florentines 126
glacé icing 27
hazelnut and chocolate flapjacks 113
low-fat brownies 106
mallow madness cupcakes 60
marbled chocolate cupcakes 76
nutty cupcakes 69
quick chocolate slices 108
raspberry and cream cheese chocolate brownies 116
rocky road cupcakes 54
truffle kisses cupcakes 67
the ultimate chocolate brownie 98
vanilla and white chocolate cupcakes 38
white and dark chocolate cookies 124
white chocolate and nut brownies 101
white chocolate scones with summer berries 87
chopping nuts 23
citrus fruit 24, 25
clementines: Brazil nut and clementine cakes 90
coconut: cherry and coconut crumble bars 117
coconut and cherry cookies 122
coconut and lime cupcakes 42
lamingtons 110
tropical fruit and coconut flapjacks 113
coffee: buttercream 27
coffee walnut whip cupcakes 49
glacé icing 27
cookies 18, 119–24
cookies and cream cupcakes 40
cooling cakes 17
creaming method 16
crumble bars 117
cupcakes 31–77
curls, chocolate 21

**D**

dainty cupcakes 51
dates: carrot traybake 100
dried fruit: fruit and nut flapjack 115

**E**

Easter cupcakes 65
eggs, preparing 14–15
equipment 10–11

**F**

fairy cakes 33
figgy fruit slice 109
flapjacks 113–15
florentines 126
frosted flowers 38
frosting, vanilla 27
fruit 24–5
fruit and nut flapjack 115
fruit cakes, testing 17

**G**

ginger: almond cookies 123
ginger and orange cupcakes 51
sticky ginger flapjacks 114
sticky gingerbread cupcakes 47
glacé icing 27
gluten-free pistachio and polenta 59
grapefruit: sea breeze cupcakes 77
green tea cupcakes 62

**H**

hazelnuts: hazelnut and chocolate flapjacks 113
truffle kisses cupcakes 67
honey: honey and yogurt muffins 89
honeycomb cream cupcakes 68
lavender and honey cupcakes 34
hygiene 28

**I**

icings 27

**J**

jewelled cupcakes 70

**K**

kitten cupcakes 36

**L**

lamingtons 110
lavender and honey cupcakes 34
leaves, chocolate 21
lemon: buttercream 27
glacé icing 27
St Clements cupcakes 35
lime: buttercream 27
coconut and lime cupcakes 42
lining tins 12–13
low-fat brownies 106

**M**

macadamia nuts: white chocolate and nut brownies 101
madeleines, apple 93
mallow madness cupcakes 60
mango and passion fruit cupcakes 58
maple syrup: carrot traybake 100
maple syrup and pecan muffins 84
marbled chocolate cupcakes 76
marmalade: toast and marmalade cupcakes 43
marshmallows: mallow madness cupcakes 60
measuring equipment 10
melting chocolate 21
meringues 15
mincemeat: jewelled cupcakes 70
mini green tea cupcakes 62
mixing equipment 11
muesli bars 105
muffins 80–86, 88–9

**N**

nuts 22–3
fruit and nut flapjack 115
nutty cupcakes 69

**O**

oats: chocolate chip oat cookies 120
fruit and nut flapjack 115
hazelnut and chocolate flapjacks 113
honey and yogurt muffins 89
muesli bars 105
oat and cinnamon cookies 122
sticky ginger flapjacks 114
oranges: buttercream 27
ginger and orange cupcakes 51
glacé icing 27
orange and poppy seed cupcakes 39
orange tuile biscuits 125
St Clements cupcakes 35
toast and marmalade cupcakes 43

**P**

papaya: muesli bars 105
passion fruit: mango and passion fruit cupcakes 58
Pavlova cupcakes 44
peanut butter: peanut and raisin cookies 122
peanut butter cupcakes 55
pecan nuts: chocolate pecan bars 102
double-chocolate brownies 97
maple syrup and pecan muffins 84
spiced carrot muffins 86
sultana and pecan cookies 121
the ultimate chocolate brownie 98
piping bags 26
pistachio nuts: gluten-free pistachio and polenta cupcakes 59
polenta, gluten-free pistachio and polenta cupcakes 59
polka dot cupcakes 57
poppy seeds: orange and poppy seed cupcakes 39
pretty pink cupcakes 75
prunes: bran and apple muffins 80
chocolate fudge brownies 111

**R**

raisins: peanut and raisin cookies 122
the ultimate carrot cupcake 52
wholemeal banana muffins 83
raspberries: raspberry and cream cheese chocolate brownies 116
raspberry ripple cupcakes 51
red nose buns 56
refrigerators 29
rocky road cupcakes 54
rolled vanilla biscuits 19

**S**

St Clements cupcakes 35
scales 10
scones, white chocolate 87
sea breeze cupcakes 77
secret garden cupcakes 71
seeds: apricot and mixed seed flapjacks 113
shopping 28
skinning nuts 22
slicing nuts 23
sour cherry cupcakes 37
sponges, testing 17
spoons 11
storage 23, 29
strawberries: hulling 25
secret garden cupcakes 71
sultanas: carrot traybake 100
spiced carrot muffins 86
sultana and pecan cookies 121
sweet shop cupcakes 64
Swiss roll tins, lining 12

**T**

tea: mini green tea cupcakes 62
testing cakes 17
tins, lining 12–13
toast and marmalade cupcakes 43
toffee: banoffee cupcakes 73
traybakes: apricot and almond traybake 107
blackberry traybake 99
carrot traybake 100
chocolate pecan bars 102
figgy fruit slice 109
lamingtons 110
muesli bars 105
quick chocolate slices 108
tropical fruit and coconut flapjacks 113
truffle kisses cupcakes 67
tuile biscuits, orange 125
Turkish Delight: be mine cupcakes 53

**U**

the ultimate carrot cupcake 52
the ultimate chocolate brownie 98

**V**

vanilla: frosting 27
rolled vanilla biscuits 19
vanilla and white chocolate cupcakes 38
vanilla crumble bars 117

**W**

walnuts: carrot traybake 100
chocolate nut cookies 122
coffee walnut whip cupcakes 49
wholemeal banana muffins 83
weighing ingredients 10
whisking eggs 15
whisking method 16
white and dark chocolate cookies 124
white chocolate and nut brownies 101
white chocolate scones with summer berries 87
wholemeal banana muffins 83

**Y**

yogurt: coconut and lime cupcakes 42
honey and yogurt muffins 89
polka dot cupcakes 57

**Z**

zesting fruit 24